Peaceful
Heart

Books by Dzigar Kongtrul

Heart Advice

The Intelligent Heart

It's Up to You

Light Comes Through

Like a Diamond

Training in Tenderness

Uncommon Happiness

Peaceful Heart

*The Buddhist
Practice of Patience*

Dzigar Kongtrul

Edited by Joseph Waxman

Foreword by
Pema Chödrön

SHAMBHALA

Shambhala Publications, Inc.
4720 Walnut Street
Boulder, Colorado 80301
www.shambhala.com

The translation of the verses of the Patience Chapter, from
The Way of the Bodhisattva (Boulder: Shambhala, 2006),
is used by permission of the Padmakara Translation Group.

Cover art: "Field Of Dreams 6" by Dzigar Kongtrul
Cover design: Daniel Urban-Brown
Interior design: Kate Huber-Parker

9 8 7 6 5 4 3 2 1

First Edition
Printed in the United States of America

⊗ This edition is printed on acid-free paper that meets the
American National Standards Institute Z39.48 Standard.

♻ This book is printed on 30% postconsumer recycled paper.
For more information please visit www.shambhala.com.
Shambhala Publications is distributed worldwide by
Penguin Random House, Inc., and its subsidiaries.

Library of Congress Cataloging-in-Publication Data
Names: Kongtrul, Dzigar, author.
Title: Peaceful heart: the Buddhist practice of patience /
Dzigar Kongtrul.
Description: First. | Boulder, Colorado: Shambhala, 2020.
Identifiers: LCCN 2020017030 | ISBN 9781611804645 (trade paperback)
Subjects: LCSH: Śāntideva, active 7th century. Bodhicaryāvatāra. |
Patience—Religious aspects—Buddhism. | Buddhism—Doctrines.
Classification: LCC BQ3147 .K66 2020 | DDC 294.3/444—dc23
LC record available at https://lccn.loc.gov/2020017030

Contents

Foreword

It may appear that we're living in exceptionally wild, heated, and unpredictable times—and in a sense we are. As each month goes by, the news of the world becomes more heartbreaking and surreal. But at the same time, much of the human experience has always been distressing, chaotic, and nerve-racking. This is because our minds tend to be in a state of perpetual struggle. We don't know what the world might throw at us next or what troublesome thoughts or feelings might pop up in our minds. And—even more alarmingly—we don't know how we'll react to whatever comes up. The only certainty, it seems, is that we will keep getting activated and making things worse. As members of *Homo sapiens*, this is one of our talents.

According to the Buddhist teachings, however, we are not stuck in this hopeless situation. This is because no human being is inherently unwholesome or confused. However we may appear on the outside, in the depth of our being every one of us is kind, compassionate, and wise. The only problem is that we lack perspective and skill in working with our stormy, tricky, and often-bewildered minds.

Dzigar Kongtrul Rinpoche has written this wonderful new book to help us gain such perspective and skill. The focus of *Peaceful Heart* is the practice of patience, which is the most effective antidote to some of our most problematic states of mind, especially anger and jealousy. This book expands on the Patience Chapter from *The Way of the Bodhisattva*, a timeless classic of Buddhist wisdom by Shantideva, an eighth-century monk who has been one of my greatest teachers and inspirations.

Shantideva and Kongtrul Rinpoche both emphasize that the main object of patience is not other people or situations but our own minds. They show us how to train in sitting still with the restless energy inside us, in being present with the irritation and resentment that makes us feel like we're about to explode. This is not a matter of grinning and bearing it but of reframing our attitude toward discomfort and learning how to relax in the midst of our own edginess.

In the more than two decades since I've met Rinpoche, he has given me many priceless instructions on how to work with my own impatient states of mind. Many of his colorful phrases and examples have stuck in my mind and made their way into my own contemplations and teachings. One of my favorites, which I borrow often and which you will find in this book, is "the propensity to be bothered." Wherever and whenever we live, no matter how perfect or imperfect our world is, working with this propensity is indispensable to our well-being. It is the only way to achieve a peaceful heart. May this book help you reach such a joyful state, from where you will be able to bring much goodness into our turbulent world.

—Pema Chödrön

Acknowledgments

This small book on peaceful heart is about how to improve our peace and sanity through the practice of patience, a resource that lies within us all. This book would not be possible without the in-depth work and sole dedication of Joseph Waxman, who put together the various talks I have given over the past twenty-five years on the Patience Chapter from Shantideva's *Way of the Bodhisattva*. I want to thank him for patiently listening to these teachings, bringing out the key points, and stringing them together in a cohesive commentary that follows each of Shantideva's verses. Special thanks to the Padmakara Translation Group for allowing us to use their translation of the verses from the Patience Chapter of *The Way of the Bodhisattva*.

I also want to express my appreciation for Jennifer Shippee, who spent many days and hours polishing Joseph's work and adding elements from outside of just the recorded talks. Since she has been present at most of these teachings and many others I have given, she was able to ensure that the written words carried my voice and expressed my intention clearly. Her efforts have brought a high level of depth and refinement to the presentation of my thoughts on this subject. I thank her for her dedication and for truly believing in the practice of patience as a genuine way to promote peace in our personal lives and in society at large.

I also want to thank and acknowledge Shambhala Publications, especially its president, Nikko Odiseos; and Matt Zepelin, the editor of this book. Everyone at Shambhala has been very open to and supportive of what I wanted this final production to be. Lastly, I thank all the students of Mangala Shri Bhuti, who have worked for hours to record, preserve, and transcribe these many hours of talks.

May this book truly bring about another way of envisioning how to work with difficult and challenging situations. May it encourage readers to turn inwardly and use creative thinking to assess and transform their mental states—especially those thoughts and emotions that destroy our well-being. The practice of patience is not easy, but throughout history it has been proven to be transformative by those who are open to its profound instructions and learn to follow them with confidence. I pray that this book may be of benefit to all who engage with it in this way.

Peaceful
Heart

Introduction

Protecting Our Tender Heart

A few years ago, I was in Varanasi, India, an ancient city on the Ganges that is considered holy in several religious traditions, including Buddhism. Every day at dusk, thousands of pilgrims come to take part in a Hindu ceremony in which they make offerings to the river to wash away their sins. One evening, I was part of the immense crowd returning from the ceremony when I noticed many people in a certain area having an intense reaction of shock and concern. When I got closer, what I saw made my heart leap out of my chest. On the pavement, in danger of being trampled, was a tiny infant, not much bigger than a melon, lying on a thin cloth. The parents had placed the baby there to attract alms. The baby was wide awake, moving, naked. My heart filled up with concern for this child. Then I realized all the people around me were reacting in the same way. All our hearts were completely occupied by concern.

What accounted for this strong common response? No one would have paid much attention to a baby doll on the ground. But this was a living being—an innocent child in a dire and painful situation, so vulnerable, so much in need of protection, stability, and improved conditions. The baby was no different from the rest of us—capable of experiencing comfort, joy, and happiness as well as discomfort, pain, and suffering. It took no time for every witness to process this. We all knew instantly that the baby was just like us, which triggered our feelings of deep warmth and care. I saw this as a reflection of the basic tenderness of heart we are all born with.

Though it is often invisible, our tender heart is with us at all times, always with the potential to come into the open and connect us to our world. The sight of the baby was an extraordinary circumstance that brought out this potential in all the witnesses. But even when we're not presented with such a compelling scene, we always have the basis for tenderness in our heart. We have the capacity to feel love toward all living beings, to care about their needs and their happiness just as much as we care about our own. This innate quality of a warm, open heart is known in Tibetan as *tsewa*. This is the main subject of my previous book, *Training in Tenderness*, but here I would like to say a little more about it, especially in terms of how it connects to the practice of patience.

For most of us in these modern times, life is full of busyness, drive, and speed. When we are caught up in this outer activity day and night, it is difficult to connect deeply to ourselves and others. Unless we want to stay in this disconnected state, we need to find some gaps in day-to-day life where we can pause and look within. These are opportunities to ask ourselves some basic, but indispensable, questions: What am I trying to achieve? Why? What am I so fixated on? Why? What exactly goes on inside me, minute by minute, hour by hour, day by day? What do I feel? What is my view of life? What are my greater aspirations?

When we can't sleep at night, or when we have a few moments to sit in a park, a quiet place, or even at the airport, we should ask ourselves such questions. Then, instead of coming up with an immediate answer, we should go a little deeper and let ourselves genuinely discover where we are. We should listen to the voice of our deeper intelligence.

I believe that anyone who pursues this kind of inner research will eventually come to the same conclusion. Beneath our ambitions and activities, what we all seek comes down to something very simple—a sense of well-being, full of joy, peace, satisfaction, meaning, and spark. We want these feelings to be with us not just for some scattered moments but all the time, without any interruptions. This means well-being can't depend solely on outer conditions. It must come from within, from a mind that is flexible, healthy, and resilient. To live in such a state of continual joy and peace is really what we're all after. This is the basic aspiration that we all have at our core—no matter how our hopes, fears, habits, and drives play out and manifest on the outside.

What can we do to fulfill this aspiration? This is not a brand-new question for anyone. We've all been working on this project our entire lives. But have we succeeded? If we had, we wouldn't have much incentive to study and practice the dharma or any other spiritual tradition. So, at this point, it would be useful to examine our old methods, to understand why they don't work, and to see if we can find a better approach.

Our habitual way of trying to achieve happiness and fulfillment is to focus our love and care on ourselves—and perhaps a few others to whom we feel connected. This is what we do most of the time. Yet all of us have also had experiences when our hearts feel much more open. We've had moments of deep warmth and tenderness toward complete strangers or even people we normally dislike.

Having had both types of experience—a narrowly self-centered heart and an open, unbiased heart—we can compare our mental and emotional well-being in the two cases. When our tenderness was focused mainly on ourselves, how much deep joy and satisfaction did we feel—even when things went our way? How did that feeling compare to our more selfless, all-embracing moments, when our kindness and compassion stretched beyond their usual boundaries? Which of these two feelings would we like to prevail in our hearts?

This is an investigation we need to do for ourselves, based on our own experiences and not just taking someone else's word for it. I've found that when my tsewa is limited to one or a few people, I suffer in a box of self-absorption. My world feels small, and my mind feels anxious. Instead of flowing freely and exuberantly, as is its inherent tendency, my tsewa becomes imprisoned by my own self-cherishing and self-protection. On the other hand, when my heart is open, I naturally feel joy, which I gladly spread to others. In summary, my personal research has led me to conclude that the main factor determining my joy and well-being is the openness of my own heart.

There is no limit to how much our hearts can open. Our tsewa can become so far-reaching and impartial that it covers all people, all animals, all living beings everywhere. We can care so much for these beings that their happiness becomes our happiness, and their pain becomes our pain. When we are filled with such deep love for others, we wish only the best for them, as a mother wishes only the best for her children. This gives our lives profound meaning, fulfillment, and joy. In this state, we deeply enjoy our freedom from the obsessive self-concern that usually plagues us.

In my own experience and from what my teachers have taught me, no positive state of mind can surpass this free-flowing tsewa. No material success, pleasure, comfort, recognition, knowledge, or "intelligence" can come close. It's not that I'm dismissing these things as unimportant. If we have tsewa, they may enhance our lives. But if the heart is closed, such things can do very little to bring about true happiness.

As we reflect on tsewa and examine it through our own experience, we may come to see it as our most precious possession. When we value something so highly, we go to a lot of trouble to take care of it. For example, most of us spend a great deal of our time doing things related to wealth. We are continually trying to gather, protect, and increase our money. This can involve working long hours, seeking promotions, watching the stock market rise and fall, searching for bargains, buying insurance policies, and so on. Each of these pursuits involves struggle, hope and fear, and suffering.

With tsewa, we also need to put effort into gathering, protecting, and increasing. We gather tsewa simply by remembering to let the heart be open, which is its natural and most joyful condition. We protect tsewa by averting and removing obstacles and threats that can rob us of this joyful state. And we increase it by training to expand our love to more and more beings.

Of these three efforts, this book is mainly concerned with protection. The obstacles and threats to tsewa come in many forms, but all arise from a heart that is in some way feeling disturbed. Something is happening that we don't like, and inside we feel some level of irritation. This could be a very subtle aggression that we may not even notice, or it could be a blatant, almost intolerable emotion that culminates in an ugly outburst of anger. However it appears, it always comes with some kind of inner rejection. We reject whatever is occurring in our lives. This means we are separating ourselves from the world and from others. When we feel aggression, the heart starts to close. Our precious, nourishing tsewa ceases its flow.

This is why the eighth-century sage Shantideva refers to aggression as "our sorrow-bearing enemy," and why I felt inspired to write a book about its antidote: patience. The word "patience" is a translation of the Tibetan word *zopa*. Other common translations are "tolerance" and "forbearance." For the sake of simplicity, I will use "patience," but the essence of *zopa* is more like "not getting disturbed."

When we are not disturbed, our hearts are at peace and tsewa flows abundantly. None of us would rather feel disturbed than be in this ideal state. But most of the time we have no sense of how not to get disturbed. We have no idea how to practice zopa, patience. On one hand, we may think that the key to not getting disturbed is to avoid any situation that might disturb us. It's common sense not to place yourself purposely in stressful or irritating situations, but it's impossible to avoid most of the countless hardships and misfortunes that come to all of us. Even people who have safe, comfortable lives usually find plenty of things that disturb them or things to complain about. This is why every Buddhist method focuses on changing our mind, not our outer world.

On the other hand, we may steel ourselves to remain undisturbed in difficult situations by mastering the approach of "grin and bear it." But that is also not what's meant by zopa. Grinning and bearing it is no different from suppressing or bottling up our emotions. It is a guaranteed method of turning the mind into a pressure cooker, which will at some point explode.

To enjoy life in an undisturbed state—what I like to call "peaceful heart"—we need to understand and be aware of how we get disturbed in the first place. Then we need to have effective antidotes for each kind of disturbance—antidotes that make sense to us and are easy to apply. These two subjects—the causes of emotional disturbance and their antidotes—make up the core of this book.

It's important to emphasize that patience is a *practice*—a practice of learning to experience feelings that are hard to tolerate without reacting in ways that cause harm to oneself or others. As with any Buddhist practice, there are many nuances and instructions for meeting different circumstances. We are fortunate enough to have an unbroken lineage of accomplished teachers who have passed on their knowledge and experience, from individual to individual, until this very day.

One of the most popular texts to be transmitted through the generations is Shantideva's *Way of the Bodhisattva*. Though it is thirteen hundred years old, its poignant and concise teachings are as relevant as ever to people of modern times. When he taught his students about patience, my root teacher, His Holiness Dilgo Khyentse Rinpoche, based most of his teachings on the sixth chapter of this work, commonly referred to as the Patience Chapter. Following the noble tradition of my teachers, instead of making up my own ideas about patience, I will take the 134 stanzas of the Patience Chapter as the framework and inspiration for everything I have to say. Thus, I hope you will consider this book to be blessed by Shantideva's own wisdom and compassion and that of all the fully realized sages who have come between us.

The word *bodhisattva* in Shantideva's title refers to a person who strives to attain enlightenment for the benefit of all living beings. Enlightenment is the state of mind of a buddha, one who has awakened to their ultimate potential. It is the most positive state of mind possible—a state of perfect, irreversible happiness and perfect, irreversible freedom from suffering. It is the ultimate state of peaceful heart, from which love flows continually and without impediment. A bodhisattva's motivation is not just to achieve this state for oneself, in order to dwell on an island of individual bliss, but to use the powerful qualities of enlightenment for the maximum benefit of all beings.

This noble aspiration is the supreme expression of tsewa. It fills the bodhisattva's life with profound happiness and meaning. This is why bodhisattvas are said to "go from joy to joy," despite being fully aware of and connected to the tremendous suffering in this world. Shantideva's intention in composing the Patience Chapter was to give people engaged in the bodhisattva path a set of thorough instructions for maintaining this supremely peaceful heart in the face of every kind of challenge and threat. My intention in writing this book is the same: to pass on any advice from my teachers that may help you work with whatever disturbances arise in your life and mind so you may meet them and use them to grow and progress on your path. I hope that by learning and applying the practice of patience, you will discover that all difficult circumstances, people, and emotions can be used to open your heart rather than close it.

ONE

Why We Need to Work with Our Anger

1

All the good works gathered in a thousand ages,
Such as deeds of generosity,
And offerings to the Blissful Ones—
A single flash of anger shatters them.

Shantideva immediately sets out to warn us about the negative power of aggression. Appreciating its potential for destruction gives us strong incentive to learn and apply these teachings. We all know from experience how unpleasant it is to be engulfed in full-blown anger, but it is worth exploring how and to what extent all forms of aggression cause damage.

If our own happiness depends on our warmth and tenderness toward others, then what can we say about a state of mind that is oriented toward harming others? As the Indian sage Padampa Sangye said, "One act of aggression is heavier than one hundred acts of desire." As an illustration, say that you see a homeless beggar on the street. You take a moment to imagine yourself in the beggar's shoes. It becomes clear to you that he wants to be free from suffering as much as you do. Immense tsewa wells up in your heart. This altruistic feeling immediately reduces your self-absorption, bringing peace to your mind. Then, if you give the beggar some money, food, or kind words—or simply acknowledge him—you experience the joy of your own warm heart. But then, suppose the beggar says or does something that offends you and you react with irritation or even anger. Immediately your positive state of mind is washed away. It's as if your compassion and generosity never even took place. The positive effects of your good heart and good deeds are destroyed, both for yourself and for the beggar. Now instead of helping the beggar, you would rather cause him harm.

We could say that feeling irritated is not quite the same as wishing harm, but unconsciously we do harbor some ill intent. Maybe we haven't formulated a wish to hurt the person who annoys us, but we have more subtle negative intentions or forms of rejection. For example, you may hope that the beggar "learns something" from the consequences of his deeds. You may feel satisfied that he got what he deserved, that justice did its job by showing what happens to a man who misbehaves. But any time you rejoice in another person's misfortune, you are annihilating your own altruistic state of mind. Any time you harbor ill will toward another sentient being, you are damaging your own tsewa.

The mind's events flow in a stream, one at a time. When the mind is negative, it can't simultaneously be positive. That would be like darkness and light existing together. So whenever we feel anger toward someone, we should examine our mind and be on the lookout for any negative thoughts or intentions that accompany the emotion. If this is too hard in the heat of the moment, we can examine our mind in the aftermath, when we have cooled down enough to have more perspective.

We can see why anger destroys peaceful heart in the moment, but Shantideva goes further than this, stating that a burst of anger can destroy "all the good works gathered in a thousand ages." How could such a large effect come from such a small cause? We can understand how this is possible by looking at how our mind and its habits can change from negative to positive and vice versa.

We may understand clearly how warmth and tenderness contribute to our own lives and those of the people around us. We may be convinced, based on the teachings and our own contemplations, that this is the truth. But that doesn't mean we can act on our wisdom in all situations. Until we've overcome all our self-centered habits and instincts, we will still be drawn to think and act against our own open heart. For a long time, our habits will retain some of their power to overwhelm our wisdom. Even longtime practitioners may find themselves being dragged back into the swamp of confusion over and over again.

The general remedy for any habit based on confusion is to develop an opposite habit based on wisdom. Shantideva gives an example of this in the eighth chapter of his book. Say you want to overcome your stinginess because you see how much it makes you suffer. When you have some food, your tendency is to think, "If I give some of this away, what will be left for me?" To counter that thought and instill an opposite, positive habit, you can instead ask yourself, "If I eat all this food, what will be left to give to others?" If you apply this antidote repeatedly, it will eventually become your first thought in this situation. The generous thought will come to you more naturally than the stingy thought. Or when both thoughts come, you can learn to go with the altruistic one and let go of the selfish one.

The path to a consistently joyful and peaceful heart depends on establishing new habits of thinking and acting for the benefit of others. This comes about gradually, through repetition. Another way of looking at this is that our transformation comes about through accumulating "good works" or, in Buddhist terminology, "merit." We can generate merit in countless ways. Shantideva's verses mention generosity and making offerings to the buddhas as two examples. But any time we open our hearts, any time we stretch beyond the limits of our self-interest, and any time we engage in the study and practice of the dharma in order to train our minds as bodhisattvas, we are accumulating merit.

Merit works in the following way. Every thought or deed of ours that is based on tsewa makes a positive imprint in our minds. As we choose to gather these positive imprints and they gather momentum, our mind slowly changes from being habitually self-centered to habitually altruistic. We also become increasingly conscious of our mind, our actions, and the relationship between cause and effect. At the same time, our outer circumstances change. The world becomes a friendlier place. Things tend to work out better for us. We feel more content with what we have and less worried. We find more opportunities to serve others, and we become more willing and able to do so. We find more opportunities to accumulate merit.

Aggression undermines this whole gradual process. Our careful cultivation of altruistic mind is derailed. It is similar to planting a tree, caring for it as it grows up, admiring it as it gets taller and taller, and then suddenly cutting it down with a chain saw. The basis of our bodhisattva path is having positive intentions toward others. But with aggression, there is a sense of wanting to bring pain or discomfort to others, generally as a result of our own pain or discomfort.

When positive intention is replaced by negative intention—when our thoughts and feelings and the basis of our satisfaction are all based on self-interest, even at the expense of others—how could anything positive remain? The traditional analogy is that we can't ride two horses at the same time in opposite directions. We can't try to be virtuous and make progress on the bodhisattva path while at the same time frequently losing our temper. Every time we act out with aggression, it not only spoils our present state of mind—as in the example of getting angry at the beggar—it also ruins the effects of many positive acts in the past, perhaps going back further than we can even remember.

The great scholar Chandrakirti compared accumulating merit to pulling a full bucket out of a well. The bucket won't come up by itself; it takes effort to bring it up to where we can drink the water. But thoughts and actions that spoil our merit are like lowering a bucket into a well, which takes no effort at all. The main effort we must make to protect our merit is in being aware of what we're habitually unaware of—our self-centered thoughts and emotions. For this, we need to practice mindfulness and self-reflection. As we become more proficient in these, we will become better at noticing when low levels of disturbance are brewing in our hearts. With improved mindfulness, we will become better at catching our irritation when it is still subtle. Before things have gone too far, we will realize we have a choice: to apply one of the antidotes from the dharma, or to follow our old habits and allow irritation to grow increasingly dangerous. Through self-reflection based on our own experience, we will become better at making the choice that is more favorable to ourselves and others.

But because of the training and effort required, it's not likely that we'll stop getting angry overnight. Does that mean we're doomed to destroy our merit as fast as we can accumulate it? If that were so, how could we ever transform our minds? Fortunately, this is not the whole story. The bodhisattva path contains skillful means for protecting our merit from our own habitual tendencies.

First, whenever we set out to do anything positive, anything for the benefit of others, we can make an aspiration that our actions will contribute to an even greater cause: to our eventual enlightenment for the benefit of all sentient beings. We can think of our action as one step toward liberation from our painful self-absorption. According to the law of karma—the natural law of cause and effect—every positive action we perform has a positive result. These actions can be physical, verbal, or mental, and their results bear fruit in various specific ways. For example, generosity naturally leads to future wealth, and patience naturally brings about physical health and beauty. But any result that doesn't reduce our self-centeredness, no matter how conventionally desirable, will not bring us genuine, lasting happiness or peace of mind. It will only be a fleeting experience without much benefit.

Therefore, we intentionally direct our actions toward something more meaningful and far-reaching, both for ourselves and for others. Joining it to the noble aspiration to attain enlightenment helps protect our merit from being destroyed by anger and other negative states of mind, such as regretting the good we have done or bragging about it to others.

Then, after we've performed a positive action, it's important to dedicate the merit to enlightenment. Dedication is a way of sealing our merit to make sure it's put to its best use, rather than bringing about short-term benefits that are ultimately meaningless. Dedicating the merit ensures that it will continue to benefit us until enlightenment. In this way, dedication protects our merit from forces such as anger.

Merit is often compared to a drop of water, which evaporates quickly if it falls on dry ground. However, if a drop of water falls into the ocean, it will last as long as the ocean does. Or, in a more modern analogy, if we put our money in a good community fund, we know that it will be used for a good cause, and we have no self-centered concern about losing it. In the same way, our enlightenment and our bodhisattva path don't belong to us: their sole purpose is to benefit others. Merit put into this "fund" is no longer in our domain, where it can be destroyed. It now belongs to a greater cause.

There are various ways of establishing our motivation and dedicating merit. For example, we can make a clear wish, in our own words, that the merit created by our actions contribute to our greater aspiration. Or we can rely on words written by the sages of the past, which come in the form of prayers. One of the most popular dedication prayers, which I and many others recite often, is:

By this merit, may all attain omniscience.
May it defeat the enemy wrongdoing.
From the stormy waves of birth, old age, sickness, and death,
From the ocean of samsara, may I free all beings.

This prayer seals our good works, ensuring that they go toward liberating all beings from *samsara*, the cycle of painful existence perpetuated by our disturbing emotions and confused reactions. By making aspirations and dedicating the merit, we protect our good works from our habitually self-centered mind and its tendency to make self-destructive mistakes. These practices also have the effect of multiplying the effects of our positive actions inconceivably.

We are fortunate to have such methods to prevent our efforts from being wasted. We should be sure to use them. At the same time, we should remember Shantideva's original intent in writing this first stanza. Anger is a terribly destructive emotion, and anything we can do to pacify and reduce it will make our lives much easier.

2

No evil is there similar to anger,
No austerity to be compared with patience.
Steep yourself, therefore, in patience,
In various ways, insistently.

The Tibetan word *digpa* is translated here as "evil." Digpa means something that makes us do self-destructive things and that jeopardizes our well-being. Nothing undermines our well-being more than anger, because when we lose our temper, we expose ourselves to our deepest vulnerability. We let loose the worst in ourselves. And when the crazed cat is let out of the bag, it's hard to catch it and put it back in. The crazed cat of our angry reactions runs around, wreaking havoc, both exposing our negative tendencies and deepening the ruts of our destructive habits.

When we react with anger, we lose our peace of mind, but even more importantly, we lose our strength. All of us would prefer to go through life in a blissful mood, laughing and smiling through our days. However, we recognize that this isn't possible. In many situations, it's not even reasonable or appropriate. We can't be ecstatic at a funeral or when we're having a serious conversation. But what we can aspire to have is a mind that is always strong. More than bliss and ecstasy, having a stable inner strength is what fosters our self-esteem the most. Our strength determines how we feel about ourselves and the world.

Our sense of strength depends on how we react to difficult situations. Think about any situation in the past when you easily could have lost your temper but instead worked to maintain your peaceful heart. How did you feel when you were able to manage your mind in such a positive way? Think about the joy of being able to save yourself and others from that danger. Didn't that give you a feeling of power and confidence in yourself? Then think about a time when you lost your patience and how that affected your own and others' well-being. If you became really angry, you may have felt all kinds of painful emotions: weakness, vulnerability, desperation, cowardice, fear, embarrassment, resentment, foolishness. Most likely, your confidence went right out the window.

Comparing these two results, it's obvious which one you would prefer. But practically speaking, it's not so easy to choose patience every time. If it were easy, the sages wouldn't have so much to say about it. This is why Shantideva uses the word "austerity." *Katub*, in Tibetan, refers to something that's difficult to do. It's hard to keep your temper, to swallow your habit of reacting. It's hard to pacify your mind, slowly and gradually, until your hot anger calms down. It feels like you're trying to tolerate something that's intolerable. It requires sitting with a deep pain in your heart, not reacting when your habit drives you to lose your temper. It requires facing your vulnerability over and over again.

Since practicing this austerity goes against our natural, habitual inclinations, we first have to reflect on what's at stake and compare the two likely outcomes. When you see for yourself the benefits of practicing patience, you will feel more determined to rouse your strength in difficult situations. The more you reflect and apply your reflection to your experience, the more inspired you will feel to face such situations. Eventually, you will even welcome these challenges. When it becomes a top priority to master patience and thus grow tremendous inner strength, you will consider it an opportunity when a friend or an enemy does something that feels like a strike to your heart. If you want your patience to become more and more reliable and steady, you will welcome that kind of pain as you do the pain of an immunization.

Having even a little bit of this confident, even cocky, attitude toward difficult experiences makes it much easier not to lose your temper. The more aversion you have toward this kind of pain, the less you'll be able to resist caving in to anger. But when you change your attitude toward this feeling of disturbance and relate to it as an immunization, when you tolerate your pain for however long it takes—five minutes, an hour, a day—that pain will turn into strength.

Until we develop this type of strength, we are vulnerable to reacting habitually. We can think, "I have to be kind, I must be kind, I must not react or lash out," but such reasoning is too feeble a remedy for challenging situations. It's like putting a small bandage on a wound that's gushing blood. A more reliable method is to keep a constant watch on our disturbing thoughts and emotions, so we can make a conscious choice about how to respond. Then we have two options. One is to let ourselves be swept away by our habitual behavior. Since we know from experience where this will lead, the alternative becomes much more appealing. Instead of succumbing to our weakness, we can joyfully practice the austerity of tolerating pain.

The pain we go through when we want to react comes from our previously established habit of indulging in anger. When disturbed, we are used to acting out in some way, discharging our pain onto someone else or onto the world as a method to release it, thinking that will make us feel better. It is painful simply to tolerate what we are feeling. There is so much momentum to react; going against that momentum feels like suddenly damming a river flowing at full force. It's as if we have to pay a price for our habit, and that price is tolerating some temporary pain. But what we gain in the end is strength.

When we know how this process works, we can have a long-term strategy for working with aggression. Every time we are faced with the possibility of getting angry but valiantly choose the option of tolerance, our mind becomes stronger, clearer, and more confident, and we take another step toward overcoming aggression as a whole. If we can learn to sit with the energy of anger or aggression that we want to discharge, that will bring us tremendous clarity, strength, and wisdom about how to proceed. Having a long-term vision about our growth gives us tremendous support in tolerating pain. We become more familiar with the experience of looking back and thinking, "I'm so glad I didn't react even though I really wanted to. I kept my mouth shut and bit my lip, and I'm so glad I did that."

As we become more and more familiar with these successes, our strength and clarity increase. Things that used to irritate us, that used to tempt us to react, gradually leave the domain of our having to be patient with them. They no longer feel like shots of pain in our heart. They don't bother us in any way. We can even enjoy them. At that point, we only have to apply patience to the bigger things, the more unusual things, the great insults to our ego, such as being unjustly accused or being attacked when we deserve to be appreciated. In the past we may have been helpless in the face of such events. It may have been impossible for us not to lose our temper. But now, even though these insults to the ego are still painful, we can tolerate them for however long we must. And eventually, as we keep gathering strength and wisdom, these major disturbances will stop bothering us altogether.

In this way, as we practice, everything gets easier. It takes less and less time for us to get over our irritations, and there is less and less residue. The whole process becomes simple and efficient. Our mind feels clear, calm, cool, and free, and our heart is at peace. Nothing may have changed in the world and our surroundings, but what has changed inside has made all the difference.

If we don't have such an approach to working with what irritates us, life can be a constant drag. Instead of changing our mind's reactions, if we try to alter our external world so we feel completely relaxed in it, we have as much chance of success as a child who tries to catch a rainbow. Once in a great while, it may appear that our world is finally set up to grant us total relaxation, but a minute later it lets us down. People who prefer to be isolated and who are in a situation where they don't have to interact much with others may be able to stay undisturbed for a while. But since the purpose of the bodhisattva path is to serve and benefit others, long-term isolation isn't a viable option. There is no way around the requirement to develop patience.

If you want to benefit others but don't know how to practice patience, you will most likely get burned out over time, no matter how enthusiastic you feel about service. This will happen not because of the terrible circumstances, but because of your own reactions. And this feeling of burnout will create repercussions of self-conflict that will further confuse and hinder you. So for anyone who wishes to serve others, whether in a spiritual or a secular way, the practice of patience is crucial. We can't work for others without feeling provoked.

Some mental strength of patience is also necessary to enable us to do other dharma practices. If you are physically ill, no one can expect you to do hard physical labor. Similarly, if your mind is distressed and reactive because you haven't been able to work through your aggression, you are not in a position to do some "higher" practice. You could pretend to do so, but your mind will be too disturbed for the practice to bear fruit. Therefore, cultivating a reflective, strong, and peaceful mind and heart through practicing patience is of primary importance if you want to practice the dharma well.

3
Those tormented by the pain of anger,
Never know tranquility of mind—
Strangers they will be to every pleasure;
They will neither sleep nor feel secure.

We all know about this from our own experience. For example, you could be on vacation in a paradise like Hawaii. You have the beach, the sunshine, the exclusive hotel, the beautiful buffet, the sheets with the one thousand thread count. But if you get into a fight with your spouse, the pleasure you felt from all of those luxuries is instantly out of reach. You can't enjoy the scenery or the food. If the fight is really bad, you may not even get to sleep on the sheets; you may be banished to the couch! All the tranquility that was there when you first arrived at the hotel has been destroyed.

When you are easily irritated, there is never any assurance that pleasurable situations will go well. Every gathering, every party, every meeting, every good time you've been looking forward to could turn into a disaster if someone says or does something you don't like or that disturbs you. You have no emotional security. Even your sleep isn't safe. If you're feeling resentment or holding a grudge, you could be in the middle of a peaceful sleep when someone pops up in your dream and you wake up pounding with anger. You may even blame the person for appearing in your dream. Then the rest of your good night's sleep is ruined.

I like the line "Strangers they will be to every pleasure" because it describes the irony of the situation. We're always working so hard for happiness, but when we let aggression take over our minds, we alienate ourselves from all the pleasures of the world.

Being habitually angry also undermines your trust. First of all, it's hard to trust yourself. At some level, you're aware that your aggression could bring you down at any moment. And since you can't trust yourself, it's hard to trust anyone else. Because your own mind is unreliable, everyone else seems unreliable as well. You are highly susceptible to paranoia. You don't know who will stick by you, who will be there in your time of need, and who will let you down or betray you.

Those who are not as subject to anger have an easier time accepting the circumstances of their lives. For example, if the economy is down or their health is precarious, they have a much better chance of maintaining their sense of peaceful heart. Those who are easily angered tend to worry more and lose more sleep over their situations. It's as simple as the simplest mathematical equation: a mind steeped in anger is a mind steeped in pain.

4
Even those dependent on their lord
For gracious gifts of honors and of wealth
Will rise against and slay
A master who is filled with wrath and hate.

Powerful people need to have capable, supportive helpers around them, because one person can't do everything alone. Those who lead countries or corporations usually need a whole staff. They may attract and encourage their underlings by giving gifts, promotions, or favors. This may steer leaders to think, "I have done so much for these people. They really owe their lives to me." But no gift is sweet enough to make up for a steady stream of intimidation or verbal abuse. When leaders or bosses lash out all the time, even those who supposedly owe them their lives will turn against them. Not many people are willing to submit to continual aggression, even when it comes with a promotion. If there is a way out, workers will take it. A gracious person may simply walk away, but most others will go on and on, usually on social media, about what kind of a person that leader or boss really is. Instead of appreciation, aggressive behavior causes the complete opposite.

5
His family and friends he grieves,
And is not served by those his gifts attract.
No one is there, all in all,
Who, being angry, lives at ease.

On one hand, you may have a big family with a grand home and an abundance of comfort and wealth. This is something many people dream of. Thanks to your past merit, you have a spouse and many children and even a large extended family nearby. But if you lack patience, your domestic happiness will be spoiled. No matter what you give them, your spouse and children won't appreciate you. You may try various means to win their affection, but your anger and reactivity undermine your efforts. Your family members learn to keep their distance. You become increasingly isolated, lonely, and disconnected. Then you may hear everyone in the next room talking and laughing, but as soon as you walk in, the whole atmosphere becomes somber. When your children or relatives pay you a visit, you know they're doing it out of obligation, and they confirm your suspicion by leaving after a short time. In so many ways, you have to endure the intense pain of rejection.

On the other hand, you may have a small family that struggles with material wealth. You have a small apartment, and everyone works extra hours to make ends meet. But if all are graced with patience, if no one has the habit of lashing out, there's going to be peace, harmony, and a strong sense of family. When other people see you together, they may actually envy you.

I used to watch the soap opera *General Hospital*. Everyone on that show is rich and beautiful. But they're all just doing their own thing, looking out only for themselves. They're reactive toward one another, with no feeling of tsewa, no sense of peaceful heart. If you ask anyone familiar with this show, "Would you like to be part of the *General Hospital* family?" they would say, "No, thank you."

It's interesting that so many of us work hard for things that don't bring us peace and happiness, but we don't make much effort to do what can actually make our lives joyful and harmonious. This verse gives us a little education about how to grace our lives and families or communities by cultivating patience.

6
All these ills are brought about by wrath,
Our sorrow-bearing enemy.
But those who seize and crush their anger down
Will find their joy in this and future lives.

We have seen a few examples of how anger burns us. If we have a lot of aggression inside, we'll constantly be confronted by our own shortcomings. Painful consequences, one after another, will keep piling up on us without a break. However, when our aggression is reduced or eliminated, we will have peace, and all our other positive qualities will blossom. As the Buddha said, "A patient person already has one foot in nirvana."

If we want to develop the strength of patience, we have to know our own weaknesses. That is the only way we can get free from them. Here is a story that really inspires me. Guru Padmasambhava, the powerful tantric master of the eighth century who firmly established Buddhism in Tibet, made many predictions about the lineage masters who would come after him. He foresaw that in the fourteenth century, a man would be born with a sword-shaped pattern of moles on his body and cause tremendous harm to the people of central Tibet. He would be like a demon. But he also said that if the man was lucky, he would meet an emanation of the bodhisattva Manjushri and then not follow the path of evil.

Centuries later, this man was indeed born and rose up to become a powerful lord. When he heard about the prediction, he identified himself as the potential demon. Not only did he have the sword-shaped pattern of moles, but he also recognized in himself a strong tendency toward aggression. At one point, he was thinking about waging war through the whole of central Tibet and was in a position to succeed. But after contemplating the results of such actions, he decided to abandon his high position and go in search of the emanation of Manjushri. When he asked people who this might be, everyone said it was the glorious teacher Longchenpa, so he sought the teacher out. This courageous and sensible response spared him and many others the consequences of his aggression. This story shows how even evil people can be redeemed through self-reflection thanks to past actions that have sown positive seeds in their mind stream. When the right conditions come about, those seeds can be activated and turn the situation around.

When we acknowledge the trouble caused by our own neurotic tendencies—in this case, aggression—we can heave a sigh of relief and start working on the antidote. But if we don't acknowledge it, no one can help us, neither ourselves nor others. This is one of the principles behind Alcoholics Anonymous, where people have to say, "I am an alcoholic," in order to overcome their resistance and start to look for a positive way out. The point is not to make themselves feel bad or depressed, but to acknowledge the situation as a prelude to seeking help to get free from their tendencies.

An important part of this process is to avoid making lame excuses for ourselves. We have to realize that excuses—even "good" ones—are not going to save us from anything in the end. Even if someone takes advantage of us, repays our kindness with abuse, or behaves in a way that everyone would agree is unjust, we are still left with our own mind, which we must find a way to soothe.

Sometimes people say, "I'm not really angry, but this is happening to me and that's happening to me, and it's not right." We can say these words and claim not to be angry while continuing to chew on our resentment. Even the best excuse will not relieve or lessen the pain of a disturbed heart. Our excuses are simply tactics to avoid confronting our self-destructive habits and neuroses. They are methods of self-delusion by which we try to convince ourselves that we don't have to change. In a sense, making excuses is a way of protecting our confusion from our own wisdom.

TWO

The Seventy-Two Ways
We Get Disturbed

7
Getting what I do not want,
And all that hinders my desire—
In discontent my anger finds its fuel.
From this it grows and beats me down.

In this verse, Shantideva begins to explain how aggression
feeds on the "fuel" of "discontent." In Tibetan, the third line
of the stanza contains the phrase *yi midewe ze*. *Yi* means "mind" or
"mental"; *midewe* means "upset" or "irritated"; and *ze* literally means
"food." When you eat healthy food, it nourishes your body and makes
it strong. But yi midewe ze only nourishes your anger. The more you
chew on this food (the more discontented you feel), the more you reject your experience and your world. Your anger keeps growing until
it gets the best of you. On the other hand, if you starve yourself of this
food, your discontented mind and its aggression will get weaker and
weaker until they eventually die.

Shantideva breaks yi midewe ze into two broad categories: not
getting what we want, which he phrases here as "all that hinders my
desire," and getting what we do not want. His commentators, however, break these categories down further into seventy-two. This list,
known as The Seventy-Two Ways We Get Disturbed, is worth becoming familiar with. Since most of the verses in the rest of the Patience

Chapter deal in some way with working with these seventy-two ways, I will describe them briefly now.

"All that hinders my desire" can be broken down into four traditional subcategories based on four types of desire. First, we want pleasure: physical, emotional, and mental. Basically, we want to feel good. Second, we want to gain wealth and material resources, which we assume will give us the means to find happiness. Third, we want to be praised. We want to hear nice things said about us, things that please us and show that we are liked. Finally, we want renown, a good reputation, a sign that we are a positive presence in the world. Whatever gets in the way of our achieving any of these four desires is yi midewe ze.

Getting what we do not want also has four subcategories based on the objects of our aversion. These are the mirror images of the first four desires. First, we don't want any physical, emotional, or mental suffering to come to us. Second, we don't want to lose our prosperity and means, which we see as protecting us from suffering. Third, we don't want to hear harsh words, blame, or criticism—anything that shows people disapprove of or dislike us. Finally, we don't want to be defamed or have a bad reputation in the world.

So far, we have eight ways of getting disturbed. The first four are based on hopes, the second four on fears. These are commonly known as the "eight worldly concerns" or the "eight worldly dharmas." But when we think about how we're affected by what happens to others—especially our loved ones and those we dislike—the list multiplies.

Just as we don't want things for ourselves, we feel upset when those we care about endure pain, material loss, harsh words, or damage to their name. Instead, we want them to enjoy pleasure, material abundance, praise, and a good reputation, and anything that hinders them from achieving these things bothers us. This category includes not only our family and friends but also anyone or anything we identify with or consider to be on our side of the fence: our teachers, religion, country, sports team, and so on.

When it comes to those we dislike—those who threaten us, those we disapprove of, or even those we generally like but who arouse our jealousy and competitiveness—we are disturbed for the opposite reasons. To me, this is a great irony. We feel upset when they have any kind of joy, when they have material success, when they are praised, and when their reputations soar. We may even feel bothered when they avoid negativity: pain, loss, harsh speech, and harm to their reputations. So when we take all the reactions based on the eight worldly concerns and relate them to the three groups of ourselves, our loved ones, and our enemies or rivals, we come to twenty-four categories of things that can feed our aggression.

We get to seventy-two when we consider that any of these twenty-four disturbances can come at us from the past, the present, and the future. For example, you can get upset by remembering how someone criticized or spoke harshly to your child last week. You can also become disturbed or anxious when you see it happening in the present or imagine it happening in the future. Multiplying the twenty-four categories by the three times—past, present, and future—we arrive at seventy-two types of yi midewe ze.*

If you put a spoonful of food in your mouth and realize it's poisonous, you will immediately spit it out and rinse your mouth thoroughly. But if you don't realize it's toxic, you'll swallow it and end up getting sick. This is just a matter of ignorance. It's not as though you want to poison yourself. In the same way, nobody really wants to experience the poison of aggression. Aggression is almost always an involuntary emotion that comes with its own force and occupies the mind. The only way we can control our aggression is by studying its causes and then not indulging in them. In other words, we have to educate ourselves about every type of yi midewe ze and then lose our appetite for them.

It's a helpful exercise to go through each of the seventy-two ways we get disturbed, starting with the original eight worldly concerns, and come up with personal examples for how they lead to aggression. I have suggested to my students that they take their time and slowly

* See Appendix B on page 211.

go through the process of matching each of the seventy-two with their own experiences. We learn so much about ourselves when we start to notice how each way causes us pain and draws us into aggression.

At first it might seem unpleasant and even painful to examine your mind in this rigorous way and possibly discover many hidden and embarrassing neuroses. So you can think of this examination as similar to a medical exam such as an endoscopy. If you have disconcerting gastrointestinal symptoms, you need a doctor to look inside you to see if anything is endangering your health. People put up with all kinds of unpleasant procedures to find out what is happening inside their bodies. But if we are concerned with our mental health and want to work with our anger, the most destructive state of mind, we also have to find out what's happening inside us. Unlike medical exams, however, once we get the hang of looking at our yi midewe ze, we will actually start to enjoy the process.

These contemplations illuminate our psychology. They uncover all the circumstances that nag our minds and eat up our peace. They lay out all the causes of our aggression, which can manifest in any form from subtle irritation to full-blown rage. When we are unconscious of the seventy-two ways, they tend to grow and spread like weeds in an untended field. But by discovering them, paying attention to them, and then applying the wisdom of the dharma, we can turn our mind into a beautiful, harmonious garden.

8

Therefore I will utterly destroy
The sustenance of this my enemy,
My foe who has no other purpose
But to hurt and injure me.

Anger comes in the guise of a friend or means of protection, but in reality, it is the worst enemy we can ever face. At times, it may seem like letting loose with anger is a great pleasure. Doesn't it feel good to let it out and really go for it? But later you find that all your peace of mind and self-respect are gone, and you feel horrible. Not only that, you've made a big mess that you now have to clean up. You have to talk and talk to repair the relationship or situation—which you may well damage again with your next bout of anger.

Sometimes aggression makes people appear powerful. They may get their way and rise to a high position by shouting and intimidating others when their demands aren't met. Many are attracted to that kind of power. But if you take a closer look, these angry people are always having to clean up their messes. They have to spend their energy making amends, giving gifts, mustering smiles, and so on. If this becomes a pattern, they find that all their mental and emotional space is being taken up by the heat of anger and its many repercussions. This makes it difficult for them to be productive and enjoy their leisure time. If they decide to keep using aggression as a tool of power and not bothering to clean up their messes, they become more and more alienated. This is incredibly painful because we are all social animals. So we should ask ourselves whether these people are indeed so strong.

Genuine strength and courage only come about by overcoming anger through destroying its "sustenance," which is none other than yi midewe ze. Mahatma Gandhi, for example, was able to free India from British rule through his total commitment to nonviolence. "They may torture my body, break my bones, even kill me. Then they will have my dead body, not my obedience." These words, which are attributed to him, show a complete fearlessness based on his having conquered aggression on a deep level. Though threatened by his oppressors with physical harm, he had no reason to fear the much more dangerous enemy of his own anger.

9
So come what may, I'll not upset
My cheerful happiness of mind.
Dejection never brings me what I want;
My virtue will be warped and marred by it.

According to our ordinary logic, we think that reacting with anger can prevent things from going wrong. We also think that if we overcome our aggression, everyone will step on us. We will be considered weak and treated with disrespect. Therefore, we need to fight to protect ourselves and get what we want in the world.

Shantideva has been refuting this way of thinking all along. He questions whether anyone has ever achieved anything positive through anger. On the contrary, hasn't our anger only made it harder to attain our goals? And what has anger done to our virtue, merit, and peace? Have these increased because of our anger, or have they been destroyed?

The dharma never encourages us to be weak or passive. A bodhisattva is not a doormat. But what we hope to achieve through anger can always be better accomplished through nonviolence and communication. This requires genuine strength, not weakness. It is much more difficult to tolerate and work with our pain than to give in to it and let it get the better of us. Working with anger rather than submitting to it gives a sense of confidence and self-esteem. And it is highly practical to go against our habits and maintain our clarity of mind so we can respond effectively to the needs of whatever situation we are in.

In this verse, Shantideva presents a direct way of working with our aggression—by cultivating nonconceptual cheerfulness. In order to do this, we must first notice our feeling of being disturbed before it turns into full-blown anger. Then, upon noticing it, we need to realize we have a choice: to feed that feeling with thoughts, justifications, and storylines, or to interrupt the process.

When we are feeling a low level of disturbance, such as mild irritation or disappointment, we tend to get trapped in the small space of our heads and make things worse by going around in circles with unhelpful reasoning. At these times, our habitual thought process usually blames our uncomfortable feelings on external events. But these events in themselves can't be the sole cause of our disturbance. Otherwise we would be just as bothered when things happened to strangers as when they happened to us. Therefore, these emotions must have another cause.

That cause is none other than our tendency to value ourselves more than we do others—in a word, our "self-importance." We are in a contracted state of mind and heart, where all our love and care is focused on ourselves or just a few individuals. In this state, if we stay in our heads and let the habitual thinking mind do what it will, our thoughts will follow their natural rut, which supports our self-importance and inflames our low-grade disturbance into outright anger and aggression. Our self-importance and its ego-centered reasoning are what spoil our "cheerful happiness of mind." I will touch more on the notion of self-importance throughout this book.

One way to get out of this rut is to do something physical that cuts through the thought process and relaxes the tension in our heart. We can try to pop out of our self-absorption simply by smiling, laughing, giggling, or taking a deep breath. We can regard cheerfulness as the gatekeeper that prevents aggression from entering the precious temple of the heart. The face of that gatekeeper is smiling or laughing.

There's a saying that "laughter is the best medicine." A doctor in India named Madan Kataria found that laughter does indeed benefit the physical heart. Since then, many laughing clubs have sprung up in India and other parts of the world. Kataria's research showed that laughter that begins artificially is just as beneficial as spontaneously laughing at something funny. Forced laughter often turns into real laughter. You can even train yourself to smile or laugh when things happen that would usually trigger the opposite reaction. I've known great teachers who have used this method. The more irritated they feel, the more they smile, and the more they smile, the more they overcome their irritations and cleanse their minds. This is a conscious process.

10

If there's a remedy when trouble strikes,
What reason is there for dejection?
And if there is no help for it,
What use is there in being glum?

Patrul Rinpoche, who taught *The Way of the Bodhisattva* frequently and extensively in nineteenth-century Tibet, liked to use the following example. If you drop your copper bowl and it gets dented, you know you can bend it back into shape. So there's no reason to get upset. If you drop your glass and it shatters, there's nothing you can do. So again, there's no logical reason to get upset. This is especially true since, as we have seen in the previous verses, getting angry only makes things worse.

To some people, it may seem like this logic is too theoretical to be useful, especially when it comes to major provocations of anger. But if you have a deep longing to get over your self-destructive aggression, and if you let this simple logic take deep root in your mind, then it becomes incredibly helpful.

His Holiness the Dalai Lama has vast responsibilities as a leader, both for Tibetans and for the world in general. Every day, he has countless opportunities to be disturbed. He has also endured tremendous hatred, oppression, and injustice. So how does he stay so consistently cheerful and poised, with such exuberant tsewa manifesting toward all beings? How does he sleep so well at night? How does he maintain his peaceful heart? He does it by thinking in this accepting way. He does whatever he can, but if there's no way for him to improve or remedy a situation, he's able to let go and maintain a calm and tranquil mind. He doesn't pretend he's a god who can change things just because he wants to.

This approach also applies to handling suffering in general. We all have to endure a certain amount of suffering. This is the Buddha's First Noble Truth; it is just how things are in samsara. Realizing there's nothing we can do about this fact of life will make it easier for us not to get so upset when things don't go the way we want.

If we look at it from another angle, however, there *is* something we can do about suffering. We can make excellent use of it to develop our tsewa and progress along the spiritual path. It can help us develop compassion for the infinite beings who are also experiencing suffering. It can inspire us to practice more so we become free from samsara and lead others to liberation. We can develop insight and wisdom by deeply investigating how and why we suffer in the first place. And as we become more tolerant of the various disturbances that arise in our lives, our patience and confidence will become stronger. Finally, having such a positive attitude toward suffering will also free us from the pain of rejecting unwanted circumstances, which is often more of a problem than the original pain itself.

11

Pain, humiliation, insults, or rebukes—
We do not want them
Either for ourselves or those we love.
For those we do not like, it's the reverse!

Here Shantideva lays out the four things that we do not want for ourselves and our loved ones, but that we do want for our "enemies," or those on the other side of the fence. This leads into the main section of the Patience Chapter, in which he gives antidotes for dealing with the seventy-two ways we get disturbed.

I've explained most of these terms in the commentary to verse 7. "Pain" refers to the first of the four categories: physical or mental suffering. "Insults" refers to the third category: harsh or critical words. Finally, "rebukes" covers anything that harms our reputation.

The second of the four categories usually refers to material loss, but here Shantideva uses a word that means "humiliation." In *The Nectar of Manjushri's Speech*, the most famous commentary on *The Way of the Bodhisattva*, Kunzang Pelden connects these ideas by speaking of "the disadvantages that come from such things as contemptuous discrimination." For example, you're on the verge of making a big business deal and earning a lot of money. Then the other party contemptuously decides that you aren't trustworthy and the whole deal is off. Any way in which another person's prejudiced or disrespectful attitude prevents you from having resources can fall under this category.

THREE

An Unconventional Approach to Our Suffering

12
The cause of happiness is rare,
And many are the seeds of suffering!
But if I have no pain, I'll never long for freedom;
Therefore, O my mind, be steadfast!

A meditation practitioner should strive to have an agile mind. Mental agility enables us to maneuver our minds in any way we like. When it comes to the seventy-two ways we get disturbed, an agile mind enables us to apply the unconventional thinking and reverse psychology of dharma. By "unconventional thinking," I mean thinking that is not based on consensus. Instead of following the general agreements of our culture or society as a guide, we follow the wisdom of the dharma, even if it goes directly against that consensus.

The goal of most conventional thinking is to preserve the ego. This is our unconscious habit and default mode. The unconventional thinking of dharma, however, aims to preserve the peaceful heart of tsewa. This requires conscious reasoning that is based on wisdom rather than habit.

The first two lines of this verse give us the reason we need to apply unconventional thinking. In samsara, the causes of happiness are vastly outnumbered by the causes of suffering. This is simply because we sentient beings have so much trouble matching our intentions to our actions. We all intend to be happy and free from suffering. We act in ways that we think will bring about this happiness and freedom, but because we misunderstand how cause and effect work, we generally bring about the opposite results. Instead of achieving the lasting happiness we all strive for, we cause ourselves and others all sorts of pain and anxiety. This is just how things are in our world of confusion. It is why the Buddha began his first teachings by saying, "Monks, this life is suffering."

Once we understand this reality, we have two choices. The first is to continue doing what we've always done, naively fantasizing about some kind of perfect existence and stubbornly ignoring cause and effect. When suffering comes around, as it usually does in some form every day, we reject it completely, not even considering that it has come about as a result of our past actions. We let disturbance take over the mind and its intelligence. Then, once in a blue moon, we may find ourselves in a place where all our wishes have come true. It's warm and sunny year-round. We have a beautiful house, glamorous friends, plenty of leisure time, and piña coladas.

Many people may read this and think, "That sounds pretty great"—and there is nothing inherently wrong with these circumstances. However, they can make us self-absorbed and oblivious to the fact that we are in samsara, where everything we would like to rely on is impermanent. Outwardly blissful states are deceptive because they numb us to this reality. We are likely to forget that we are on the road to old age, sickness, and death. If that happens, we will miss our opportunity to develop a tender heart and transcend self-absorption. This is why the teachings consider birth in one of the heaven realms—where pleasure is at its peak and pain is virtually nonexistent—to be a grave misfortune.

The other choice is to use unconventional thinking. Instead of reacting toward our pain with anger, we embrace the pain by seeing it as the key to our ultimate freedom. Without suffering, we will never understand how sad samsara is—both for ourselves and for all sentient beings. We will remain under samsara's spell, its false promise of happiness, and lack the inspiration to see through its illusion. This disenchantment with samsara, called *kyoshe* in Tibetan, is the root of our determination to seek a path to liberation. It is what gives us the strength to keep going in the face of obstacles, and the perspective and discernment to make wise choices when confronted with samsara's temptations. Without kyoshe, we will never become free of the attachments that bind us. Therefore, any pain that promotes our kyoshe is something to celebrate.

Usually we are caught up in our ego's world, which we're always trying to expand and protect. When we notice this happening, we can either tighten the grip of ego, or we can try to see suffering in new ways. By choosing to use our suffering to help us become free of samsara, we start to withdraw from the world of ego. We become more curious about what is going on inside. This process of self-reflection frees us from ego's grip. Then we can begin to see the causes of our self-destructiveness, the main one being self-centered aggression.

A few hundred years after the time of the Buddha, the glorious emperor Ashoka ruled most of the Indian subcontinent. He had expanded his ego's kingdom in a way that few people in history have. Then one day he noticed that a Buddhist monk was giving teachings to one of his wives, who treated the monk with great devotion. Ashoka became extremely jealous and decided to have the monk executed right away. But the monk showed no fear. This confounded Ashoka, who had been in many battles and had never seen anyone, not even the bravest warrior, show such fearlessness. The intense emotional pain of jealousy that Ashoka suffered and the intriguing mystery of the monk's fearless mind made the emperor turn inward and self-reflect. He realized that there was a different way of looking at life. This monk had something important to teach him. So he started to receive teachings from the monk's own teacher and eventually became one of the greatest patrons of Buddhism the world has ever known.

Unconventional thinking and reverse psychology are like secret weapons in our battle against aggression and fear. When we come to adopt the attitude of seeing all adverse circumstances as blessings, we have nothing to fear or reject. There is no longer anything to worry about because we can turn whatever happens to us into a means of growing further. This gives us tremendous confidence as we go through life.

When we study the lives of the buddhas and bodhisattvas of the past, we find that they all had the mental agility to make good use of difficult circumstances and suffering. It is said in the teachings that peacocks can eat food that is poisonous for other beings. Instead of making them sick, the poison makes their feathers brilliant. In the same way, when bodhisattvas encounter the seventy-two types of disturbing food—yi midewe ze—the practices they apply make their patience brilliant. This leads them out of the suffering of samsara and into the peace and bliss of enlightenment.

13
The Karna folk and those devoted to the Goddess,
Endure the meaningless austerities
Of being cut and burned.
So why am I so timid on the path of freedom?

Here, Shantideva is referring to Indian rituals of his time, which he believed did not lead to ultimately meaningful results such as liberation from samsara. It is easy to come up with modern-day equivalents. For example, people risk their lives and go through great ordeals just to say, "I climbed Mount Everest." Because they feel inspired, they willingly face great pain and risk.

On a more mundane level, look at what so many of us do to achieve wealth, success, or fame. In Japan, many young people who want to advance in their corporation work almost around the clock and sleep in their office to save time. I find this to be amazing. There is no guarantee that they will rise to the top, and even if they do, what is the ultimate benefit? But modern society's consensus tends to support such extremes of hard work—as long as one has a conventional aim such as making millions of dollars or winning an Olympic gold medal.

Artists, on the other hand, have to justify their existence unless they are able to make a living from their art. Society in general does not respect aspiring or unknown artists. It is a similar situation for Buddhist practitioners. It is hard for others to see the benefit of your practice and to appreciate how you are spending your time. However, if you justify your existence based on the approval of others, you will feel insecure and frustrated as a practitioner.

Therefore, it is important to emphasize self-respect. Respect toward yourself is more significant than any respect from others because you know yourself better. When you practice patience, for example, you must know why you're doing it and how it benefits you. If you value self-respect and do virtuous things that are unknown to others, you will naturally gain self-confidence, strength, and freedom from your neuroses. You will feel more and more inspired to develop your tsewa and shed the eight worldly concerns because of the benefit and freedom you personally experience by doing so. Your heart will be at peace, and eventually others will respect you as a person who has truly been transformed.

14
There's nothing that does not grow light
Through habit and familiarity.
Putting up with little cares
I'll train myself to bear with great adversity!

We can't become patient, tolerant people simply by thinking we should be patient and tolerant. We have to train ourselves, starting with how to handle small irritations. Once these become easy to deal with, we'll be better equipped to be patient in more difficult situations.

There's nothing that doesn't get easier the more you do it. For example, when you first learn how to drive, it seems so overwhelming. You have to handle the wheel, the pedals, and the gears. You have to read all those signs and be aware of so many cars, pedestrians, and police officers, not to mention your GPS and your phone. Your life and the lives of many others are at risk. It can be absolutely terrifying. But now you just get in, start the car, and go. You don't even think about it.

When I see what people become used to, I'm often in awe. Look at how difficult it is to be a farmer, a medical student, a Marine, a mother of small children. When you've never done these things before, they seem almost impossible. But people do them and do them very nicely because they've gotten used to these situations.

Similarly, as we become familiar with the practice of patience, as we train ourselves in bringing the remedies of the dharma to heal the disturbances brewing within, we find it easier to forgo anger and remain in a state of mental peace.

15
And do I not already bear with the common irritations–
Bites and stings of snakes and flies,
Experiences of hunger and thirst,
And painful rashes on my skin?

16
Heat and cold, the wind and rain,
Sickness, prison, beatings—
I'll not fret about such things.
To do so only aggravates my trouble.

If we look at our lives, we already have a certain amount of patience. We can bear many difficult circumstances quite well. For example, we all have to endure minor illnesses such as colds and headaches. We have to deal with plenty of weather we don't like. We put up with mosquitoes and mice and many other creatures that cause us minor trouble.

Rather than constantly seeking to eliminate all small irritations from our lives, we can use them as a basis for developing more patience. If you emphasize comfort over the practice of patience, your mind will get weaker and weaker. If you want your life to be free of the challenge of needing patience, your mind will be in constant fear. You will feel increasingly under threat, increasingly provoked, increasingly paranoid. This will lead you to act more and more negatively and to reject much of the world.

Practitioners need to be going in the opposite direction. We need to have a little oomph to work with all the challenges we encounter. A lot of people wonder, "Why does my life have so much struggle?" But there is no such thing in samsara as a life free of struggle. There is no such thing as a life where nothing threatens us. So instead we should ask ourselves, "Why doesn't my life have more oomph?"

It's interesting that it's easier to be patient with things or beings that cannot be held responsible, such as the weather or infants. We should also notice that it's relatively easy to muster our tolerance toward people we want to please or impress, such as those we find attractive or our superiors at work. These examples show how capable we are of having control over our minds. If we use these easier situations as a training ground, we are also capable of extending our patience to situations or people that tend to provoke our anger more strongly.

Shantideva's point here is that developing patience depends a lot on our self-confidence and self-image. If we see ourselves as nervous, shaky, and irritable, our experiences will tend to follow that image. So we need to change our attitude to see ourselves as tolerant and not easily disturbed. This will make a great difference in how we react to outer conditions and will set in motion more favorable ways for things to unfold. When we see ourselves in such a positive light, it will be easy to tolerate small disturbances, let go, and move on with ever-increasing patience. As our minds become more agile and ready to make use of discomfort and adversity, we will gain more and more strength to face the great disturbances of life with tolerance.

17

There are some whose bravery increases
At the sight of their own blood,
While some lose all their strength and faint
When it's another's blood they see!

18

This results from how the mind is set,
In steadfastness or cowardice.
And so I'll scorn all injury,
And hardships I will disregard!

Our reactions to situations, people, and our own states of mind are based on how we condition our minds. For instance, if you have habituated yourself to be brave in battle, seeing your own blood flow may give you even more courage to fight. But if you've habituated your mind to weakness and oversensitivity, you may faint or panic even when you see someone else's blood. Your response in that moment comes from how you've built up your habits in the past.

You can train your mind to be strong and resilient, or you can train your mind to be fainthearted and easily discouraged. This is your choice. If you want to be a bodhisattva, it's not viable to act like a weak dog and run away with your tail between your legs, succumbing to your habitual reactions. A bodhisattva needs to endure countless challenges, so you have to shed any tendencies toward cowardice.

In these modern times, particularly in the West, it's common for people to give up on themselves easily. Many dharma students tend to judge themselves too harshly and then become discouraged. Part of the problem is they want to be too good. So when they see their neuroses and their imperfections, they have a hard time accepting themselves. This comes from having unreasonable expectations. It is a puritanical mind-set. I hear people say, "I've been practicing for the last twenty years. How could this happen? How could I do this? How could I have this thought, this feeling?" This often happens just when they think they've made some progress. The result can be deep despondency.

Our thoughts, feelings, and reactions come about due to a vast number of interdependent circumstances. When the perfect circumstances converge for you to have a particular reaction, it's almost impossible not to have that reaction, at least initially. As a result, no matter how long you've practiced, it's very unlikely that nothing will bother you anymore. It isn't realistic to think you'll be exempt from getting frustrated or losing your temper. The mark of a true practitioner is not what arises in your life and mind, but how you work with what arises.

It all comes down to your perspective and your self-confidence—your *oomph*. Now you may think, "What can I do about that? I'm just not a self-confident person." It's important to know that self-confidence isn't something we're born with. Everyone can develop self-confidence if they want to. But we must understand that here we are talking about genuine self-confidence, not ego's bloated version, which is more like arrogance.

The process begins with your willingness to take a chance. Rather than having everything absolutely clear and predictable ahead of time, you have to be willing to go into the unknown. This may require a leap of faith—faith in your own mind and its innate wisdom and ability. Then, having taken that leap, you have to work with your intelligence—skillfully, mindfully, and patiently—as the situation unfolds. Going through this kind of process repeatedly will increase your self-confidence, especially when you encounter difficulties and find ways to turn them around or bring about the best outcome possible.

Here it is helpful to remember verses 15 and 16, in which Shantideva advises us to train ourselves in cultivating positive qualities by beginning with relatively small things. This is a realistic, doable approach to developing any desirable attribute in your mind. For example, you may wish to be a generous person but realize that you're not very generous. Resigning yourself to being stingy by nature will get you nowhere. That is just making an excuse based on laziness.

If you're genuinely interested, you can always find small ways to be generous. You can even practice by passing money or some object you're attached to from one of your hands to the other. The Buddha actually suggested this simple practice to a disciple who thus got over his miserliness and eventually became a great patron of the dharma. Starting small will serve as an effective beginning to your generosity practice, which you can then take as far as you want it to go.

With patience especially, we can use the small irritations that come up in our lives as wonderful opportunities to train. For example, sometimes we feel offended, but at the same time we realize it's silly to be offended. Here we have a great chance to apply the humor we already see in the situation. This humor is based on realizing the irony of what is happening: we're blaming somebody else, but the real problem is our own ego, manifesting in the form of a ridiculous uptightness. This kind of ironic humor is not just a patch we use to cover up pain. It is an insight that can turn irritation into a genuine laugh or smile, which gives us a feeling of release. A humorous perspective gets us through the slight pain of the offense and enables us to turn that pain into wisdom. We can then appreciate the pain as we would the pain of an immunization. We need to take advantage of these situations, which are within our reach to work with successfully. If we forgo such opportunities to practice in small ways, then to believe we will be patient when bigger things come around is just wishful thinking.

Because humor and appreciating irony are such effective means of cutting through irritations, I would like to share a contemplation I once had, which I found both funny and helpful. It occurred to me that people come with different shoe sizes, but that doesn't bother me. They have different pants sizes and hat sizes. That also doesn't bother me. So why should I be bothered that people come with different sizes of ego? Just as I don't have to wear other people's shoes, I don't have to wear other people's egos. I can just let them wear their own egos, whatever size they are. Why should I take the size of someone else's ego personally and let it bother me? It is theirs and theirs alone to wear. I can just let them be.

The size of another person's ego can make you feel very bothered and uncomfortable. But if you can find other ways of looking at your irritation, especially using humor, then you have a better chance of being patient. In this way, your patience will increase not only in trivial situations but also in serious situations where humor and irony are more difficult to find.

19
When sorrows fall upon the wise,
Their minds should be serene and undisturbed.
For in their war against defiled emotion,
Many are the hardships, as in every battle.

When it comes to outward actions, such as battles, some people are naturally stronger and braver than others. But here we are talking about an inner battle—the battle not to let our emotions, especially aggression, control or get the better of us. We are talking about the battle to protect our warm, tender heart from what threatens it most. In this sphere, we all have the ability to increase our inner strength and bravery. The main requirement is to see the value of making an internal change. This comes from understanding how patience is crucial to our well-being. Once we are convinced of this, it's not hard to take the necessary steps.

In this verse Shantideva mentions "the wise," by which he means those who have learned ways to make their hearts peaceful, whatever the outward circumstances. The wise know how to keep their cool. They have markedly diminished their propensity to be bothered because they appreciate the people and events that try their temper as practice opportunities. They have room for such appreciation because of the skill they have developed in applying unconventional thinking in the way we've been discussing.

Many people, however, have a resistance to unconventional thinking. To regard as positive something conventionally seen as negative seems like manipulating, bypassing, or simply being unsympathetic.

But the willingness to use unconventional thinking—particularly this method of turning things around—is a key component of the practitioner's makeup. If you prefer just to stick with conventional views and approaches, then why study spiritual teachings? Why not simply go along with the consensus or do what feels right at that moment? In the case of being bothered or disturbed, what generally feels right at that moment is to react with anger—either outwardly or at least mentally. Why not continue to do that?

We should know that the basis of being a practitioner is to work with the mind and resolve things within ourselves rather than focus on changing outer circumstances. Knowing this, at least on some level, is what makes us seek teachings and teachers. It's what makes us learn and appreciate the dharma. This kind of unconventional thinking is one of the main ways by which we can improve our internal environment. The better we get at using it, the more it will become our instinctual response to whatever disturbs our mind.

By "instinctual response," I don't mean that we will never get angry. Wise dharma practitioners may still get irritated and even let out some words of aggression. But they catch themselves and recover their footing quickly, and from there they move confidently toward a better solution. Even when faced with pain in the midst of struggle, they know they can overcome it by applying the wisdom they have understood and practiced. Some may think this approach is unnatural or contrived, but this is how the practice of patience can become a reliable strength. Their growing sense of confidence gives these practitioners a joyful sense of anticipation about working through difficult circumstances. They are "wise" because they know the difference between wisdom and neurosis, and they always side with wisdom. With this perspective, they have no reason to reject anything that comes up in their lives. They can see all situations as ways for them to learn, grow, and progress.

In this, we should again start by practicing in small ways. Work with seeing small setbacks and annoyances as blessings. Gradually learn to see how unfavorable experiences contribute to your spiritual progress. We have an incredible saying in Tibetan: *Yo na yo ga, me na me chi.* This means, "If you have it, it's a great joy. If you don't have it, it's a great blessing." Applying this kind of philosophy will help you always see that the glass is half-full rather than half-empty. If you can take this to heart, you will eventually develop a sense of contentment and appreciation in all situations, regardless of outer conditions.

20

Thinking scorn of every pain,
And vanquishing such foes as hatred:
These are exploits of victorious warriors.
The rest is slaying what is dead already!

Shantideva uses a lot of battlefield language because he came from the *kshatriya*, or warrior, caste in India. Here he uses it to make a comparison. In ordinary battle, the more you slay people, the more your enemies will increase, and the more people you will need to kill. This mind-set quickly turns into a total loss of sanity because your enemies increase endlessly. Since there is no way to slay the whole world, the killing goes on forever. Therefore, killing your enemies is completely pointless—as pointless as slaying a corpse, as the second half of the verse says.

Most wars are like the Tibetan story of the two friends who set out on a nice journey to Lhasa. At one point, they sit down to enjoy some tea and get into a conversation. Soon this develops into an argument. They are so furious that they start hitting each other. An old man comes along and says, "Stop! Why are you hitting each other?"

They answer, "We can't agree on how to divide these five gold pieces."

"What's the problem?" inquires the man.

One of the friends exclaims, "This guy says, 'I take one and you take one, and I take one and you take one, and I take one!' That means he'll get three, and I'll get only two!"

An Unconventional Approach to Our Suffering | 47

The other friend chimes in, "Well, he says, 'I take one and you take one, and I take one and you take one, and I take one.' Then *he'll* get three!"

"This really isn't such a big deal," the old man says. "You could just break the last piece in half. Now, where are the gold pieces?"

The friends respond, "Well, actually we don't have any. We were just hypothesizing." I don't mean to sound mocking, but most of our geopolitical problems are something like this.

In contrast to this absurd scenario, striving for victory over our self-destructive emotions, as it states in the first half of this verse, has great meaning. If you conquer your own aggression and vanquish all your habitual tendencies to be provoked, you have overcome the deadliest enemy in the entire universe. The result of this victory will always stay with you, and the warmth of your heart will flow freely for the tremendous benefit of yourself and others.

21

Suffering also has its worth.
Through sorrow, pride is driven out
And pity felt for those who wander in samsara;
Evil is avoided; goodness seems delightful.

When we are hit with suffering, it seems like something terrible is happening. But often, when we have come through the experience, we look back and realize that this suffering has helped us change for the better. This verse describes a few ways in which suffering can benefit us.

People who are proud or arrogant often don't realize how much pain they are in. Their pride blinds them to the fact that they are constantly in the uncomfortable mind-set of judging others and thinking they are better in some way. They think they are more honest and genuine, that they have all the answers. This makes them uninterested in what other people think or say. Although the emotion of pride makes them feel high, such a high is always in comparison to others, who must then be relatively "low." The constant effort to maintain their superior status comes with deep insecurity. Anyone who appears to be catching up or simply doing well becomes a threat. All of these factors cause arrogant and prideful people to become isolated from others—if not socially, then at least on a deep, internal level. In this state, it is difficult for them to open their hearts and enjoy the warmth of their own innate tsewa. For such people, pain is sometimes what softens them. Being unexpectedly hit with internal suffering such as depression or illness may make them more humble and open to those around them, whom they once judged harshly. They start to appreciate others more and seek out their advice or help.

Another benefit to being hit with pain or suffering is increased compassion for others. When you experience your own suffering, you can sympathize more genuinely with what others are going through. At other times, though you may understand and even empathize with the suffering of others, you don't know the real taste of that suffering in your own mouth. Even if you care for people, you can't quite connect to their experience personally, even if you want to. So undergoing your own suffering can make you more sensitive to others. As a result, you become more careful not to harm them and naturally more inclined to do things on their behalf.

When your suffering is caused by your failure to work with your own anger, instead of rebuking yourself and then sinking into low self-esteem or guilt, you can use your pain to develop compassion. The first step is to forgive yourself. Remember that you didn't lose your temper because you wanted to. Like all beings, you value your peaceful heart and experience your deepest joy and peace when it is flowing freely with tsewa. No one who has a sense of their naturally warm and tender heart prefers to burn with anger. And those beings who are cut off from their own tsewa and rarely experience the warmth of their hearts suffer most of all. They live in a cold, dark state of ignorance, oblivious to the most precious treasure they possess.

The suffering of anger, aggression, rejection, and extreme self-protection is not just your own suffering. It is the suffering of all humanity and all sentient beings. You can forgive yourself for having the same afflictions and reactions as all other beings. You can feel compassion for your own ignorant state of mind. Your ignorance and the habitual reactions it produces are a universal feature of sentient beings. So when you overreact or fail to apply the patience practice you have learned, you are better off if you forgive yourself and feel self-compassion. In fact, if you hope to fully develop the immeasurably loving capacity of your heart, you must forgive and feel compassion for yourself. Otherwise, how can you have positive thoughts and emotions toward others?

Even if you recognize that you repeatedly fail to practice patience because you are too sensitive and overreactive, remember that humanity as a whole is too sensitive and overreactive. Your habitual tendencies are the tendencies of humanity. Or if you are close to someone whose skin is like a balloon full of air, ready to pop, and you frequently bear the brunt of their anger, remember that humanity as a whole is temperamental and volatile. This is why we have so many conflicts and wars that last for lifetimes, generations, and even centuries. Understanding that the person who is always getting mad at you is just a regular human being caught in human tendencies will help you transform your resentment into compassion—not only for them, but for all of humanity. It is painful to have an unreasonable, hypersensitive mind, but this is what you and all people have, at least from time to time.

When someone harms you, it is of course extremely difficult to open your heart to them. When someone has harmed you repeatedly and unjustly, it may even seem impossible. But here it is important to reflect that the point of forgiveness is not to give a gift to the one who has harmed you. In fact, that person may not even be seeking your forgiveness. The point is to give a gift to yourself. What the other person has done to you may well be unjust from a conventional point of view. But whether it's just or unjust, do you want to be held hostage to that anger for the rest of your life?

Most of us have suffered injuries and traumas that are stored in our brains, our bodies, and particularly our hearts. When similar conditions arise, these injuries generate fear, rejection, aggression, and unconscious patterns of harmful behavior. Even if we understand the value of opening our heart, when the pain of deep wounds comes up, we can't simply bypass it and maintain a state of free-flowing tsewa.

The only way to move forward is to let your deeper wisdom take ownership of your life. You have a conscious choice—to remain a hostage to the past or to move forward, as difficult as that might be. The latter choice will involve coming to understand that we all have habitual tendencies that make us susceptible to harming others. If you rouse the courage to move forward in this way, you will eventually be liberated from your past wounds and have a clear path to a bright future.

The conflicts we have with each other are universal conflicts. Reflecting on that will help you transform your own suffering into compassion for all humanity. In so doing, you will also find your mind becoming calmer as you gradually remedy your unconscious habit of anger and replace it with the conscious habit of compassion.

Suffering can also inspire you to learn more about the actual causes of suffering, as well as the causes of happiness. If you've been studying the dharma, then you have heard that suffering comes from attachment to the self. But this knowledge may seem remote and theoretical until your suffering pushes you to look into it more deeply. Now, thanks to your suffering, you have something at stake in genuinely understanding these teachings. You have a personal reason to connect the dots of cause and effect. As a result, you become driven to self-reflect more deeply to understand what is happening in your mind and emotions. From there it is natural to abandon actions and mind-sets that cause suffering and to adopt actions and mind-sets that lead you away from suffering. Your eyes really begin to see samsara as a whole, to see the endless cycle of painful existence in which all sentient beings are trapped. This may compel you to take a wider look at your life and think more deeply about how you choose to spend your time. Does it still make sense to prioritize this small, individual self and let your unconscious habits run your life, or would it be wiser to focus on gathering, protecting, and increasing your tsewa?

It often happens, for example, that people who are driven by the desire for wealth and success have a change of heart after going through a depression or major loss. For the first time, questions arise: *What am I going to do with all my money and possessions when I die? What will I do with my position, my power, my reputation? What use is it to anyone else or even to myself?* At that point, people may be moved to connect more to their open hearts. They may then donate some of their time and assets to churches or charities. Their suffering can change the focus of their lives from the small, individual self to a more altruistic way of being, which ultimately can bring greater satisfaction. In the best case, that altruism becomes directed toward finding a way to liberate ourselves and all other living beings from samsara. Then it can even develop into the quest for enlightenment.

Across the globe, for centuries upon centuries, people have had a universal, shared sense of what is good: everyone knows that it is good to be generous, to do positive things in the world, to benefit others. Those who partake in such activities have tremendous joy in their lives. For the most part, they have more self-worth and satisfaction than those who live only for themselves. In our heart of hearts, we all want to be part of this universal good. But our self-interest often blinds us to our deep desire. So sometimes it is only when we encounter suffering that we actually tune in to our longing and turn our minds toward achieving our greater potential, which is why Shantideva almost praises suffering in this verse.

FOUR

Is There an Agent? Deeply Analyzing What Brings Us Pain

22

I am not angry with my bile and other humors—
Fertile source of suffering and pain!
So why should living beings give offence?
They likewise are impelled by circumstance.

23

Although they are unlooked for, undesired,
These ills afflict us all the same.
And likewise, though unwanted and unsought,
Defilements nonetheless insistently arise.

24

Never thinking, "Now I will be angry,"
People are impulsively caught up in anger.
Irritation, likewise, comes
Though never plans to be experienced!

Verse 21, in the last chapter, may have been only partially convincing. You may say, "Yeah, I see how suffering can help me grow and develop good qualities. But it's still hard not to get angry with people who harm me." So now Shantideva asks us to look closer at what makes us angry. Do we get angry with our illnesses?

A condition such as heart disease may cause you intense agony, but do you get angry with the heart disease in your own body? Similarly, a natural disaster such as an earthquake or a tsunami may bring devastation to millions of people, but how many of them get angry with the physical elements that caused it? Does it make any sense to get angry at the earth or the water?

But then you may say, "I'm not talking about diseases or elements or anything without a mind. I'm talking about people who have a mind, who have intentions. I'm talking about people who harm me intentionally." This thinking shows what hurts us the most. We think there is a conscious agent, willfully acting to harm us. If that "agent" is someone we've loved and cared for—someone from whom we expect respect and reciprocation—such treatment can really break our heart. It can also cause trauma and lead us to feel paranoia and a fear of entering close relationships. We don't know who might deliberately turn against us, and we don't feel we could handle something like this happening again.

This line of thinking, however, is based on a misunderstanding, a belief that there is an autonomous person who is in control. But consider this. Just like a disease or an earthquake, a person's actions are based on many causes and conditions coming together. It is not generally the case that they have a clear intention to hurt you. They are often driven by their own emotions, such as anger. There is no actual intrinsic agent.

Reactive thoughts and emotions that arise in our minds generally determine our behavior and what comes out of our mouths. We have no control over what arises in our minds from moment to moment; it depends on circumstances. Most of the time we behave decently, but in some situations, we can't help losing control and hurting others, even when we have every intention not to.

The arising of anger can be compared to the arising of an image in a mirror. An object placed before a mirror has no intention to produce a reflection. Nor does the mirror have any intention to reflect it. But the meeting of the two is a sufficient cause for an image to appear. In the case of anger, there is the meeting of the provoking circumstances and the person who is provoked. The circumstances that provoke the anger have no prior intention to do so. And the mind that reacts has no prior intention to be provoked. But when the two come together, anger arises. This is how habitual, unconscious reactions are generated.

Here it is helpful to look at your own experience of being angry. When your anger comes up strongly, are you in control? Are there times when you intend not to lash out but find yourself doing so despite yourself? When you hurt people out of anger, are you an autonomous agent with evil intent? Or does it sometimes feel that you are overpowered by your reactive mind and emotions? Looking openly and honestly at yourself in this way gives evidence that no one who acts out in anger is in control.

If we see how this happens in our own minds when we lose our mindfulness and awareness, we will understand better how anger grips the minds of other people and drives them to do hurtful things. Having this view will make us more tolerant of others' unkind actions. It's our habit to assume there is an autonomous agent harming us, just as it's our habit to assume that a bus going down the street must have a driver. But in this case, it's as though the bus has no driver.

It's also important to consider that when you are on the receiving end of someone else's anger, that person is generally suffering more than you are, especially once you come to understand this view of "agentlessness." You are more conscious of what is going on, are able to self-reflect, and have a clearer choice not to succumb to your habitual tendencies. The other person most likely does not have these advantages. Being unaware increases one's suffering many times over—both in the present and as a result of indulging in actions that have severe karmic consequences for the future. If we understand this, we can turn the harm done to us into an opportunity to let go of our resentment, forgive, and start to feel warmth toward the other person. In this way, we can shift a situation that we thought was beyond the possibility of change and use it to help us develop universal tsewa.

25

All defilements of whatever kind,
The whole variety of evil deeds
Are brought about by circumstances;
None is independent, none autonomous.

26

Conditions, once assembled, have no thought
That they will now give rise to some result.
Nor does that which is engendered
Think that it has been produced.

These verses encourage us to examine in a more subtle way whatever makes us angry or irritated. Looking into our assumptions and projections about the objects of our anger will release us from the tendency to react strongly against them. Whatever provokes our aggression—a person, a situation, our own mind—must seem real to us. Otherwise there would be no reason for us to feel threatened by the object and to react with anger to protect ourselves.

Our sense of an object's intrinsic reality is not based only on concepts or thoughts; it is even more than an emotional sense. It is, rather, a deep-seated unconscious belief in the true existence of things, which animals have just as much as humans do. Based on this belief, our emotions arise continuously. To break down this belief and the resulting emotional thrust that projects an object's reality, we can start by investigating our belief with reasoning.

Anything that we consider real must have three characteristics. It must be singular, unchanging, and autonomous. Since this is a very important reflection that we can make use of again and again regarding any physical or mental object, I will take a moment to explain it here. "Singular" means it is one thing, as opposed to a collection of parts. "Unchanging" means it stays the same from one moment to the next. "Autonomous" means it exists on its own, independent of other factors. These are the ways in which we unconsciously believe or hold on to things as real, intrinsic, truly existing.

It is obvious that everything is made of parts, but when we are in the grip of a strong emotional reaction, we fail to make use of this knowledge because our unconscious belief has not yet been penetrated by that knowledge. If our unconscious beliefs or assumptions have been penetrated even a little bit, it becomes harder to hold on to our anger, even when it arises as a reaction. If we were fully aware that the object of our anger was a collection of parts, it wouldn't make sense for us to feel anger toward that object as a whole. That would mean being angry with every part of the person, situation, or source of irritation. But, in the case of a person, we don't usually have a problem with their eyebrow or knee. So which part would be reasonable to focus on as the object of our aggression? Perhaps the brain or the heart? If it's the brain, which part of the brain? Does it make sense to say you are mad at a particular part of someone's brain? Even if you are mad at one brain part, that part can be further divided down to the atomic level. There are trillions and trillions of atoms in each human body. Does it make sense to get mad at an atom or a certain group of atoms? Does it make sense to be pissed off at something too small to see? And if you can't find even one atom to be angry with, how can you be angry at something that is made of those atoms?

Perhaps you agree that there's no specific body part with which you should be angry. It's the person's mind that is the problem. But the mind is not a physical object; it is insubstantial. At the same time, it has many aspects: thoughts, feelings, and perceptions. Therefore, the mind is not a singular thing. Understanding this, which aspect of a person's mind would you choose to get mad at?

If you get mad at their thoughts, consider that thoughts come in chains, like the beads of a mala, which seem like one long entity but in reality are not. When we look into our own mind and try to identify a thought, we notice that our past thoughts have vanished and our future thoughts haven't arisen. Only the present thought is here. But when we look at the present thought that is seemingly here now, we find that it is very hard to pinpoint. We can know what we are thinking, but trying to catch our present thought is impossible. The actual thought dissolves as soon as it arises. Every event in the mind arises and dissolves simultaneously. This is just how things are for everyone and everything if we take the time to investigate. So having done this analysis, the question is: what are you left to be angry with?

Now let's look at the second assumption, that the object of our aggression or irritation is unchanging. In this case as well, our habitual emotional reactions blind us to our own knowledge. We all know that everything changes. We witness the seasons change; we witness children growing up and adults growing old. Yet in many ways we still hold on to a sense of permanence. For example, we believe that the "me" of today is the same person as the "me" who was born decades ago. But even yesterday's "me" is not the same as today's. We have probably all heard that seven years from now all the cells that are in our bodies today will have been replaced. Even though I am told that this information is not completely accurate, the fact remains that innumerable cells in the body are being born and die every day. These changes are too subtle to notice, but we can clearly perceive how much our bodies change in a year or more.

On the most subtle level, every split second is a fresh moment. Every instant, subtle changes take place in the body and mind. In the last twenty-four hours, every person alive has changed, from instant to instant, an inconceivable number of times. Therefore, yesterday's problem, threat, or enemy is, in reality, not here today. In our minds, we tend to hold these situations as static, but actually everything is ephemeral, impossible to nail down no matter how hard we try. If we deeply understand and maintain our awareness that things have no permanence from moment to moment, we will find it difficult to remain upset about anything for long.

The third assumption we can be sure we're making when we get angry or irritated is that the object is autonomous. In other words, we assume the object exists "from its own side"—meaning it exists independently of conditions, whether or not there is a subjective viewer. This assumption, or deep belief, is the main subject of these two verses. If we didn't make this assumption, it would be impossible to react to anything or anyone with aggression. Looking closer at this idea, it is easy to understand that nothing is autonomous. A plant needs water, sun, nutritious soil, and many other things in order to exist. It also requires a subjective viewer to confirm its existence. No plant exists self-sufficiently in a vacuum. This is true of everything in the world.

Everything is the effect of causes and conditions. Effects must have causes. They don't arise because they want to arise; they have no volition of their own. Things can only happen when all the right causes and conditions come together; as soon as one of these is absent, the effect can no longer be there. Furthermore, each cause and condition has its own prior causes and conditions. If you try to trace back all the causes and conditions, you will never find the beginning. You also won't find a simple linear progression. Since everything has multiple causes and conditions, trying to trace things back only reveals how complex this or any given situation is. This is an extremely helpful exercise, which Shantideva prescribes in several places in *The Way of the Bodhisattva*. The universe is a vast network of interdependent connections. So, of all the countless causes and conditions leading up to this current threat to your well-being, which one would you focus on? Picking just one to react to would simply be an arbitrary choice.

For any effect that you observe, it's also important to realize that *you* are one of the causes and conditions. You play an important role in bringing the situation about. Say someone has criticized or snubbed you, and now you are hurt and angry. You were hoping for pleasant words to enter your ears, but instead you got unpleasant words. This happens to people all the time, but it is rarely something we look into more deeply. In this case, analyze the causes and conditions. First of all, your hope for approval is one of the main reasons you got as upset as you did. That's one cause. Then, perhaps the other person didn't give you that approval because they felt pressure to do so. You yourself don't like to give others your approval when you feel pressured. In fact, it makes you rebel and do—or at least feel—the opposite. So in this situation, you can actually sympathize with the person who did that to you. Or maybe the person criticized you with a good intention in their mind. For example, they noticed the awkward dynamic you have with the world and wanted to point it out for your benefit. They saw how emotionally sticky you are, how overly dependent on what others think. They saw your potential to become more self-reliant and self-confident and used this opportunity to help you make a shift. Even if they lacked the skill to help you break through this dynamic, the good intention was still behind it. What is the basis of your anger here? Can you be angry at their good intention? Can you be angry at the sound of their words? At the meaning of their words? At their thought process? At your own reactiveness?

There are so many factors that it makes no sense to focus your aggression on a single one. And if your aggression has no focus, it has no chance to build and lead to more aggressive thoughts and actions. After doing this investigation, there may be a residual feeling or sensation for a while, but if you've reasoned with yourself and reflected on these points, the great danger of mindlessly indulging in aggressive behavior will be averted. On the other hand, if you don't investigate in this way, your thoughts will probably run along these lines: *This person is really not on my side even though they should be. Instead of showing me the loyalty and affection I'm due, they are actually trying to hurt me. And how can they be criticizing me when they have this fault, that fault, and all those other faults? Who do they think they are?* And so on. In this way, each thought you add to the story in your mind adds fuel for your anger to get hotter and hotter.

So when you get angry, take a few deep breaths and try to be silent and reflect on the causes and conditions. Be curious to determine which ones come from you and which come from the other person. Look into the causes of those causes. Take this important opportunity to look into which of the seventy-two ways you are getting disturbed. Have some awareness of the greater objective, which is to protect your precious tsewa. And then, instead of going to either of the two extremes of indulging in the emotion or trying to suppress it, simply rest your mind in that open, self-reflective state. Because your investigative wisdom has brought you closer to the truth of the situation, your mind will probably be in a more peaceful state. The truth is often the best remedy for a turbulent mind.

In the earlier example, there is the truth of your needing approval, that need becoming a pressure for the other person, their rebellion against the pressure, their deeper intention, and all the causes behind this scenario. Acknowledging all this as true will be like putting a cup of cold water into a pot of boiling water. Immediately your mind will calm down. On a deeper level, there is the truth of your investigation that sees the illusory nature of all we hold to be real—or singular, unchanging, and autonomous. Just rest in that open, present, self-reflective state.

This process is called *che gom*, or analytical meditation. If you can use your mind in this way, you will have fun on your meditation cushion, even when working with anger or resentment. Sometimes the best practice time is when you are confronted with strong emotions that have previously overpowered and bewildered you. While out and about, you're not able to penetrate them because things are moving by too quickly, but when you sit on your cushion and reflect deeply, you get to the bottom of what is going on. By looking for and not finding something singular, unchanging, and autonomous, you come to realize the truth: that the object of your anger is illusory. In this way, you release yourself from that emotion, which has been keeping you hostage. This is one of the most joyful experiences of practice.

Even before you get to the cushion, you can anticipate this joy. Instead of just reacting by picking up your phone and lashing out with a text message, you can set your intention to make your way to the cushion and work things out there. Then you can spend half an hour getting to the bottom of your experience. If, after the half hour, you still need to send that text, you can do so. Since most of the harmful and destructive things we've ever done have happened in the first half hour, if you pick up the phone at this point, you will be much safer.

You won't be getting into the ring with your boxing gloves and shorts on because most of the problem will have already been resolved in your mind. This is what it means to bring your life to the practice cushion and integrate the dharma into your day-to-day experiences.

In all of this, begin by training with small things and then train with more complex situations that have many sides to them. But even when things are quite complex, you usually have an intuitive sense of the many sides involved, and you usually know the best course of action. The training here is in bringing that innate wisdom to the forefront and using it to clarify your mind.

Sometimes you will find that others can shed light on your situation and help you break down the causes and conditions and how they've come together to put you in a bind. Asking for the perspective of others who have been in your situation and know it more fully can give you helpful hearing wisdom. But then you need to contemplate for yourself. Decide whether what they're saying is true and whether it corresponds with your experience. The person advising you is not necessarily innately gifted in this field. Whatever clarity they have around this issue has probably come from years of experience. You can train yourself to have an equal level of clarity by taking time to contemplate on your own.

It's important to pay attention to your more subtle aggressive thoughts because they can keep coming up and causing you problems for a long time. Even thoughts coming out of a mild level of irritation or resentment can return again and again. For example, you may have an encounter with someone and have the passing thought, *That person's arrogant.* The thought enters your space of mind and dissolves, and you move on. But the impression left by that thought remains. You might not see the person for twenty years, but as soon as you catch sight of them again—before you've even spoken to them—you have the unconscious sense that they're arrogant.

Thoughts have tremendous power to leave lasting negative impressions and form unconscious attitudes toward things. Unless you cultivate the habit of paying close attention to what's going on in your mind, you won't be aware of many of these impressions. And unless you connect the dots and realize how unkind thoughts about others damage your tsewa and disturb your peaceful heart, you won't make any effort to cleanse your mind. Without this conscious cleansing, no negativity will go away on its own. The way to cleanse your mind is through conscious investigation. Ask yourself, *What did I perceive? How did I react? Was it necessary for me to react in the way I did? Why did I react? What was triggered?* This will help you notice your impressions and subtle attitudes and let go of them.

Mindfulness, self-reflection, and analytical meditation are powerful methods to undermine our habitual reactiveness. As we keep pursuing our investigations, the potential objects of our aggression start to feel less solid. When we reach a certain level of proficiency, we can be in the presence of what used to bother us without even having to resort to investigation. We will simply be less bothered by our world and others. Doesn't that sound nice?

27

The primal substance, as they say,
And that which has been called the self,
Do not arise designedly,
And do not think, "I will become."

28

For that which is not born does not exist,
So what could want to come to be?
And permanently drawn toward its object,
It can never cease from being so.

29

Indeed! This self, if permanent,
Is certainly inert like space itself.
And should it meet with other factors,
How could they affect it, since it is unchanging?

30

If, when conditions act on it, it stays just as it was before,
What influence have these conditions had?
They say that these are agents of the self,
But what connection could there be between them?

In these verses, Shantideva debates with non-Buddhist schools that believe in permanent, autonomous entities. One of these, the Samkhya school, believes in a "primal substance" that is the cause and makeup of everything, as well as in a conscious, autonomous self known as *atman*, which is the unchanging essence of every being. In accordance with the commentary for verses 25 and 26, we can think of the atman as a more formal version of our deep-seated, unconscious belief in a singular, unchanging, autonomous self.

If we are looking for something intrinsic in our enemy to blame, this atman would seem to be a good candidate. But if we want to hold the atman responsible for any harm done to us, we should first investigate whether it is actually capable of producing emotions that lead to harmful behavior. The atman never changes. Its emotions such as anger, on the other hand, rise and fall. Anger is not a permanent part of the atman; it comes and goes due to particular causes and conditions. The atman itself can't be one of those causes and conditions because it's always the same. If it were a cause of anger, then anger would always be present, which is clearly not the case.

A permanent, autonomous atman has no power to affect anything else. In fact, it can't act at all. Since it never changes, it can't act in one way today and in another tomorrow. It can't do something now and then stop doing it five minutes from now. For if its actions did change, what would determine that change? The atman would have to be influenced by causes and conditions. But something affected by causes and conditions is not autonomous. This argument demonstrates that any permanent, autonomous entity has no ability to affect other things. In this way, such an entity is similar to space, which is inert and static.

Like everything that takes place in the mind, anger comes about through dependent origination. There is no willful, autonomous "self" making it happen. No one feels angry or acts out in aggression simply because they want to. We are all vulnerable to the causes and conditions around us. How we feel, what we do, and our intentions behind our actions are all subject to countless factors, which are also constantly changing. Therefore, when we think someone is consciously trying to harm us, we are making projections that have nothing to do with the reality of interdependence. No one acts as willfully and free from influence as we think they do. By contemplating in these various ways whoever or whatever seems to threaten us, we can learn to get a better handle on our own angry and resentful reactions.

If you find a poisonous snake under your bed, you try to remove it as quickly as possible. If you leave it to its own devices, sooner or later it will bite you and you will suffer pain or death. Aggression is like a poisonous snake lurking in the darkness, but instead of harming you just once, it harms you many times every single day. Anything that repeatedly arises in your mind as a threat can provoke you to self-destructive aggression at any time. Therefore, it is prudent to apply these antidotes in a timely manner, just as you would remove a snake under your bed. Here it's important to remember that we are speaking of working with our minds and our own habitual reactions internally. At the same time, we must continue to observe the laws of karma and the conventional world.

31
All things, then, depend on other things,
And these likewise depend; they are not independent.
Knowing this, we will not be annoyed
At things that are like magical appearances.

The wish to attain enlightenment in order to guide all other sentient beings to enlightenment is known as *bodhicitta*, a Sanskrit word that means "mind-set or heart of awakening." We all have the potential for this noble attitude because we all have the innately warm, tender heart of tsewa. The main subject of Shantideva's book is how, from this common basis, we can gradually cultivate bodhicitta until it is completely merged with our being, and we attain our highest potential and become fully enlightened beings, or buddhas.

Bodhicitta has two inseparable aspects, known as "relative" and "absolute." On one hand, we cultivate relative bodhicitta using the conceptual mind. For example, by thinking about the deep and endless suffering of sentient beings, we inspire ourselves to attain enlightenment so we can liberate them from samsara. Absolute bodhicitta, on the other hand, is based on wisdom beyond concepts. It comes about through direct insight into the nature of phenomena. This insight, when it is completely unobstructed, enables our compassion and our ability to benefit others to blossom to its fullest extent.

The first eight chapters of *The Way of the Bodhisattva* focus on relative bodhicitta, with Shantideva's teachings on absolute bodhicitta mainly reserved for the ninth chapter, known as the Wisdom Chapter. However, the Patience Chapter also touches on the absolute, so it is important to talk about that a little here.

As we become adept at using analytical meditation to investigate whatever provokes our aggression, irritations, resentments, and grudges, we will find that the practice gradually transforms our ordinary perceptions and emotions. This training in seeing the interdependence of all phenomena has the effect of making things start to lose their feeling of realness and weaken their grip on us. Especially in formal practice, we begin to see and react to whatever arises as more like rainbows. A rainbow is a magical appearance that arises when sunshine, rain, and moisture in the atmosphere come together in the presence of a viewer who is in a particular time and place. Like rainbows, all phenomena and experiences are products of interdependence. They are insubstantial and without essence, leaving us nothing to hold on to, nothing to react to, nothing to pinpoint.

Another way of saying this is that rainbows and all other phenomena are "empty." But this doesn't mean they are nonexistent or void. Rainbows appear in the sky vividly. There is nothing about them that resembles a void or vacuum. Similarly, all interdependent phenomena—people, places, emotions, our own bodies, and so on— appear and function. Yet at the same time, when we look deeply, we can't find anything stable and solid to hold on to or pin down. Nothing is singular, unchanging, and autonomous. Therefore, nothing has any essence to pinpoint. This is what Shantideva and other Buddhist sages are talking about when they use terms like "illusory" and "empty." When one has a direct, nonconceptual realization of emptiness, that is absolute bodhicitta. It is important that we know this as an experience on our meditation cushion, not just intellectually.

Shantideva's Wisdom Chapter treats the subject of emptiness rigorously, engaging in debates with Buddhist schools that have less complete or refined views of the empty nature of all phenomena. A deep presentation of emptiness is beyond the scope of this book, but the brief contemplations in this verse and elsewhere in the Patience Chapter can serve as stepping-stones to realizing absolute bodhicitta. For now it is helpful just to investigate the nature of all appearances that we unconsciously believe to be real by seeing if we can identify a singular, unchanging, autonomous essence.

When we do this again and again, we come to see personally what the teachings mean when they say that all appearances are like rainbows and all events of our lives are like the events in a dream or a movie. Any sense of reality is merely a result of our habitual projections and beliefs, which are rooted in ignorance. When we wake up to the illusory, interdependent nature of all things, not only will we free ourselves, but we will also see how other sentient beings suffer so much. Full of genuine compassion, we will then have no greater desire or aim than to help free others from their ignorant, habitual projections.

32
"Resistance," you may say, "is out of place,
For what will be opposed by whom?"
The stream of sorrow is cut through by patience;
There is nothing out of place in our assertion!

Having contemplated the previous verse, you might now think, *The object of my patience is just like a rainbow. I, the person who would like to be patient, am like a rainbow as well. My aggression and the remedy of patience also have no reality to them. So, what's the point of all this? How can this practice have any effect?*

This is all true in the context of the absolute nature of things. Ultimately, anger and patience and the people involved are empty of any solid essence. But we have not yet realized that absolute nature. We operate based on our obscurations, on our clinging to the self and the phenomenal world as real. In the context of how things appear to us and how they function in our relative world, patience is an important tool for reducing our suffering and furthering our progress along the spiritual path. Shantideva is saying we should practice patience because it works. It reduces our suffering.

When studying the dharma, it is easy to confuse the absolute and the relative and mix contexts. Shantideva uses this verse to address this confusion. Guru Padmasambhava, the great enlightened master who established Buddhism in Tibet, gave a simple guideline for navigating absolute and relative: "My view is higher than the sky, but my attentiveness to actions and cause and effect is finer than flour." Here, "view" refers to the ultimate way of seeing things. It is the perspective that the true nature of all phenomena is emptiness. But without fully realizing emptiness, it would be foolish to act as if our actions didn't matter.

How we conduct ourselves is, in fact, one of the most important factors in our ability to comprehend the absolute truth. Whenever we react with aggression, we reinforce the idea that there is something real to be aggressive about. When we apply patience, however, our hearts become peaceful, which gives us more room to be able to see the illusory nature of things.

33
Thus, when enemies or friends
Are seen to act improperly,

Remain serene and call to mind
That everything arises from conditions.

Enlightened beings are those who have realized completely and beyond any doubt that all things that appear are illusory, like the example of the rainbow. This recognition includes all phenomena from tables and chairs to planets and stars. It also includes all mental phenomena, such as thoughts, emotions, and perceptions. But by far the most significant aspect of their wisdom, which brings them the greatest personal freedom, is that they no longer have any belief—conceptual or emotional—in an intrinsic self. Thanks to their thorough efforts in analysis and meditation, they have concluded—without any lingering uncertainty or doubt—that there is no real "I" that needs to be cherished with attachments and protected with aggression.

As we have seen, in order to grasp at anything as real, you must have the unconscious, deep-seated belief that it is singular, unchanging, and autonomous. Without reflection, this self appears to have all three characteristics. Even though you know you are made of parts, you have the sense of being one unit, a singular individual, "me." Even though all aspects of your body and mind change continuously like a flowing river, you feel there is an underlying "me" that never changes. And even though every aspect of your being is based on and governed by myriad causes and conditions, you consider yourself to exist as an autonomous person. But deeper analysis—as we have already discussed in relation to potential objects of anger—reveals that no such self meeting these criteria exists.

If we do these investigations for ourselves—if we look for an intrinsic self in this way or any other way and never find such a thing—we will be liberated from the tyranny of ego. The ego is also not an intrinsic thing. It is more like an ignorant habit, a habit of grasping to an "I" that can't be found. From this habit comes the tendency to cherish and protect the "I," depending on the situation. This then brings about all the disturbing emotions that keep us bound within samsara. But those who have realized the illusoriness of "I" have shed the ignorance that perpetuates this habit and tendency. Thus, they have exhausted all possible reasons to get caught in painful emotions.

Aggression, for example, is a direct result of believing in an intrinsic self. When we believe in such a self, we identify completely with it and consider it the most important thing in the world. When it seems to be threatened, we have an immediate impulse to protect it. This impulse naturally comes with aggression in order to push away or eliminate the threat.

In this verse, Shantideva suggests that when anything happens to provoke our aggression or even our aversion, we reflect on the interdependent nature of all phenomena, including this self. First, this "I" that demands to be protected, as we have already seen, depends on myriad causes and conditions. Furthermore, our enemies and loved ones also lack an intrinsic existence of their own. Considering things in this light, it is difficult to identify one thing to get angry at or attached to, despite our initial reaction and the pull of our habitual response. Even the emotions have no substance to pinpoint as truly existent. Therefore, the whole experience of aggression or attachment is just like a dream—a dream that will continue until we wake up to the empty nature of all things.

The point is that we can see the irony of how we hold on to things in contrast to how things really are when we investigate them, even just a little. Along with showing us this irony, which naturally breaks up the solidity of our reactiveness, this practice naturally opens our hearts and gives room for our tsewa to flow. By seeing and getting some distance from our own misunderstandings about reality, we come to realize how these misunderstandings are universal.

It's not only we who are caught up in these ways. All sentient beings are similarly caught and similarly have a constant longing to be happy and free from suffering. At the same time, all of us, no matter how we appear on the outside, have the potential to become fully enlightened. But we all dwell, for the time being, in the darkness of ignorance and confusion. We can sympathize with this universal predicament because we ourselves live in it and feel the impact of our misunderstandings many times every day.

This sympathy serves as the ground in which we can cultivate bodhicitta. Two of the greatest methods for generating and strengthening bodhicitta are the contemplations on loving-kindness and compassion. Loving-kindness is the wish for other beings to be happy and to have the causes of stable, deeply fulfilling happiness. The ultimate form of happiness is to realize and completely merge with one's own enlightened nature. Compassion is the wish for others to be totally free from suffering and all causes of suffering. The ultimate form of this freedom is to be entirely rid of ignorance, especially the mistaken belief in an intrinsic self. This state can only be attained when one realizes and completely merges with one's own enlightened nature.

Therefore, the contemplations on loving-kindness and compassion naturally point toward the ultimate wish for other beings to attain enlightenment. And since it is necessary for beings to have guides who can show them a path to enlightenment, we feel inspired to become enlightened ourselves in order to become such guides—not because we are better than them, but because we have a little head start, having encountered the liberating wisdom of the Buddha's teachings.

Recognizing the universal predicament of sentient beings also serves as an antidote to our habitual biases in favor of certain individuals and against others. Usually our feelings about people are based primarily on our own self-cherishing and self-protection. Based on who we think we are and what we think we want and don't want, we have "friends" and "enemies." We like some beings, dislike others, and feel indifferent toward the majority. But contemplating how all beings, including ourselves—in fact, using ourselves as examples—are identical in their constant wish to find joy and avoid pain, makes it easier to shift the focus away from our exclusive self-interest and to start caring about others' needs as if they are our own.

We can further strengthen this unbiased view by reminding ourselves that all beings have the potential to become enlightened. The Buddha taught that enlightenment is our true, innermost nature, no matter how we temporarily appear or act. It is the birthright of every sentient being: whether we are human beings or animals, altruistic or selfish, peaceful or vicious, intelligent or stupid, we possess an enlightened nature just as a mustard seed possesses mustard oil. Our enlightened nature underlies everything else.

Our constant striving for happiness and freedom from suffering is a sign that we are dimly aware of having such a nature. On some level, we are all aware that it is possible to attain a state of perfect, irreversible happiness and perfect, irreversible freedom from suffering. Even though this is propelling us forward every minute of the day, our present striving in samsara is based on cherishing and protecting a self. This in turn is based on the mistaken belief in an intrinsic self. This belief, and the habitual tendencies that spring from it, are the very obstacles that prevent us from enjoying and becoming one with our enlightened nature. Not only that, they prevent us from enjoying much of our ordinary lives. But our mistaken belief is impermanent and can be eliminated through the practice, such as by doing the contemplations we have been speaking of.

All the characteristics that differentiate sentient beings appear temporarily because of causes and conditions—our past actions, our habitual patterns, our environment. When those causes and conditions change, the characteristics also change. The only thing that remains with us at all times—that always lives within each of us, at the very core of our being—is our innately enlightened nature. For this reason, we are all equal in our potential. Every one of us is destined to become a buddha.

One of Shantideva's main ways of remedying aggression is by applying sound reasoning. Most of his arguments in this chapter are easy to follow and hard to refute. But when we are angry, we don't always want reasoning, even if it makes sense to us. Instead of wisdom, we would rather have our emotions, however painful they are. We can be addicted to our emotions the way some people are addicted to substances. When addicts are given their desired substance, they can muster little or no resistance. Thus, they often abuse the substance until it knocks them out or incapacitates them. We often show a similar inability to work with our emotions intelligently. We find ourselves overwhelmed—at times even possessed—by them, swamped in confusion and immune to the wisdom that we know to be true.

As an antidote to our weakness, we must continually set and reset a strong intention to work with our aggression. Without being hard on ourselves, we must think, *If I don't work with my anger and aggression, I will ruin any chance I have at deep happiness and well-being. I will destroy my fragile shoot of bodhicitta before it can develop into a tree that offers abundant flowers and fruits to others. Instead of becoming a precious guide to beings, I will continue to do them harm and accumulate negative karma for myself. Therefore, I must prioritize wisdom and find ways to delve deep and apply what I've learned to my day-to-day experiences of life.*

To support this resolve, it is helpful to spend time around people who are patient themselves. Observe them and learn how they do it. What is their attitude? How do they apply wisdom in circumstances that would make you quite disturbed? How do they come out the other side of a challenging encounter with their hearts still open and present—and without sweeping things under the carpet?

Study them as if studying a text. In this way, their good qualities and peaceful hearts will start to rub off on you. Simply appreciating, admiring, and being open to these people can significantly undermine our tendencies to react with anger, because we know there is another way. But in order to do any of this, we have to be willing to change. We have to be willing to let go of our emotional addictions and become the wise, present, honorable, kind, patient people we would like to be—and can be.

FIVE

Widening Our Perspective on Adverse Circumstances

34
If things could be according to their wish,
No suffering would ever come
To anyone of all embodied beings,
For none of them wants pain of any kind.

35
Yet carelessly, all unaware,
They tear themselves on thorns;
And ardent in pursuit of mates and goods,
They starve themselves of nourishment.

36
Some hang themselves or leap into the void,
Take poison or consume unhealthy food,
Or by their evil conduct
Bring destruction on themselves.

Now Shantideva moves on to another type of reasoning. Here he is pointing out how little control we sentient beings have. Not one of us wants to suffer. All of us, without exception, long to be free from suffering and its causes and conditions. But despite this ever-present intention, we are constantly bringing suffering upon ourselves. What is it that keeps sabotaging our longing for peace and happiness? What is it that keeps drawing us toward the pain we wish to avoid? What makes us harm ourselves and others? It is nothing other than our mistaken belief in an intrinsic self and the actions that unfold from this belief. This is what the Buddha taught.

This mistaken belief is the source of our aggression and all the other emotions that wreak havoc in our lives. These emotions undermine our intelligence and make us vulnerable to causing ourselves all kinds of harm. Romeo and Juliet, for example, both kill themselves because of the confusion that results from their deep attachment. Many people work themselves into a state of great stress and ill health because of greed. Addicts seek pleasure or a respite from pain, but their substance abuse multiplies their suffering. People go to war and are killed by the millions because of aggression. Similarly, jealousy and pride cause us to think and act self-destructively, despite our overall intention to be happy and free from suffering. Sometimes these emotions and the actions that go with them appear to bring benefit or relief, but that is only temporary. In the long run, there are always painful repercussions. These examples, along with those given by Shantideva, all demonstrate how helpless we are in the face of our unbridled, afflicting emotions.

37
For when affliction seizes them,
They even slay themselves, the selves they love so much.
So how can they not be the cause
Of others' bodily distress?

We are so vulnerable to our afflicting emotions that we will even harm ourselves while under their influence. Since this occurs even with our beloved selves, it is only logical that our afflicting emotions will drive us to harm others as well. Again, this is not because of any clear thinking or willful purpose. It is just that aggression, desire, jealousy, and pride—if left unchecked—have the power to blind us and take away any resistance to behaving in a harmful way.

When we are in intolerable emotional pain, we don't often remember that everything arises interdependently, due to countless causes and conditions. Instead, we tend to fixate on one cause and direct our anger there. In this confused state of mind, which has narrowed down to focus on that one thing, it is difficult not to act out with aggression, which may even bring about bodily harm. We have no control: the emotion's influence is too strong, and our resistance is too weak. We have not yet built up the strength and momentum of reflecting on the causes and conditions that make some things come about.

38

Although we almost never feel compassion
For those who, through defilement,
Bring about their own perdition,
What purpose does our anger serve?

If we are on the bodhisattva path, we must generate compassion for beings who are so blinded by ignorance and caught up in their afflicting emotions that they harm themselves and others. We should not hold them to be autonomous beings with total control over their body, speech, and mind. There is no point in reacting to them as if they have a clear intention to harm us, for that is not the case.

39

If those who are like wanton children
Are by nature prone to injure others,
There's no reason for our rage;
It's like resenting fire for being hot.

40

And if their faults are fleeting and contingent,
If living beings are by nature mild,
It's likewise senseless to resent them—
As well be angry at the sky when it is full of smoke!

If you want to be a good kindergarten teacher, you can't expect the children to behave like adults. You have to assume that they will behave normally for their age. Otherwise, you will easily get impatient and be an ineffective teacher. The situation is similar for aspiring bodhisattvas who live in samsara. In this world, we sentient beings are largely driven by our self-interests and frequently overcome by our emotions. The Buddha referred to beings with this mind-set as *sipa soso kyewo*, or "childlike, individually oriented beings." This is not an insult; it is simply a way of describing the reality of the situation. Until we go completely beyond our mistaken belief in an intrinsic self, we will always behave—at least from time to time—like children.

For example, if one person is in a higher position than the other, the higher one tends to feel proud and condescending, while the lower one tends to feel inferior and envious. Among equals, such as colleagues on the same level, there is often a mutual feeling of uneasy competitiveness. From these emotions, many small and large irritations rise to the surface, often leading to unkind words and actions. For childlike beings, as for actual children, this is a natural course of events.

Living among childlike beings puts us in many situations where we have to work with aggression—both our own and that of others. But this is also an ideal training ground for practicing patience and for the bodhisattva path in general. It is said that bodhisattvas from different realms choose to be born in our world because it offers such splendid opportunities to train one's mind. In more peaceful places, such as the celestial realm of Dewachen, it is much less common for one to be provoked. But in our world, anger and aggression arise as naturally as the heat of fire. Bodhisattvas feel that kind of heat and can still be burned, but they welcome the fire as a basis for deepening their practice. They don't run away or try to avoid such circumstances. Nor do they indulge in an ordinary mindless way, becoming caught up or blinded. They use each circumstance as an opportunity to train their minds through the very same reflections and investigations we have been discussing.

One might feel moved to consider the absolute teachings that say the true nature of sentient beings is like the sky. From this point of view, our ignorance and the harmful emotions and actions arising from that ignorance are dependently originated and fleeting. They are impossible to pinpoint or characterize. In other words, they are empty. These faults are like smoke in the sky. They are separate from the sky and can do it no harm. Whether or not smoke is present, the sky always remains the same—pure and stainless.

Shantideva also holds this ultimate view of the true nature of beings. But this only strengthens his argument that there is no reason to get angry when they do us harm. Their skylike nature is not what threatens us. It is the fleeting and contingent smoke, which is unrelated to their essence and is not who they truly are. How does it make sense to get mad at someone when what we are mad at is not who they are? Furthermore, if our own nature is also like the sky, how can the smoke of someone else's faults cause us any real harm?

41
Although it is their sticks that hurt me,
I am angry at the ones who wield them, striking me.
But they in turn are driven by their hatred;
Therefore with their hatred I should take offence.

Here Shantideva presents a very refreshing piece of reasoning. If someone beats you with a stick, you don't get angry at the stick because you don't hold it responsible. You see that it has neither the will nor the autonomous power to hurt you. You know that the stick must have a person operating it, so you hold that person responsible and you get angry at them.

But, like the stick, the wielder of it is in the grip of a controlling force, which is anger. This anger makes the person vulnerable and out of control. It takes away the person's ability to act with a clear intention. From this point of view, it would make more sense for us to get angry at the anger that drives the stick-wielder.

We can take this a step further by looking at the anger itself. Anger is not autonomous. It only appears in the presence of causes and conditions. The most basic requirement is for the person's self-protective tendency to be provoked by a perceived threat. But this tendency also has a cause, which is the mistaken belief in an intrinsic self. Ignorance is the root of the whole process. It is the root of samsara, and it is an affliction that harms everyone, including ourselves. How could we hold an ignorant person responsible? The word "ignorance" itself tells us why this makes no sense; it means "not knowing." How can someone be blamed for what they don't know? That would be like blaming a blind person for not knowing that your hair is brown.

If we ponder this logic and apply it to our experiences, we will convince ourselves that there is never a sound reason to get angry at anyone. We will continue to react and occasionally lash out, but this is a result of our own habitual tendencies, which also have their basis in ignorance. But training the conceptual mind in this manner will gradually work away at the habitual tendency to be reactive.

42

In just the same way in the past
I it was who injured living beings.
Therefore it is right that injury
Should come to me their torturer.

On the night the Buddha attained enlightenment under the bodhi tree, he was visited by demonic forces who wanted to prevent him from achieving his complete realization of the truth. They shot arrows and knives at him, but the weapons turned into flowers. Because the Buddha had purified and exhausted all the negative karma from every one of his lifetimes, there was no way harm could come to him. And because of the kindness and compassion he had developed over many lifetimes, the sharp weapons became gently falling flowers.

We have not yet reached the purified state of the Buddha, so we have large amounts of unpaid karmic debt, or *lenchak* in Tibetan. In our past lives, and even in the present one, we have harmed countless beings, knowingly and unknowingly. Each harmful action sows a seed in our mind stream. Later—perhaps many lifetimes later—this seed ripens into some form of pain for us when the appropriate conditions come together.

We may think, *Why is this person harming me as opposed to harming someone else?* The reason is that we have inflicted pain on that being in the past. This is the only explanation that could account for why we are now the "victim," whether or not we can remember what we did. Most likely, we have gone back and forth with each other, alternating as victim and aggressor, over many lifetimes. We are equal in this: both parties are equally at fault, equally vulnerable, and equally ignorant. By acknowledging our part in this drama, we can release ourselves from the need to react with a new round of aggression. This is the only way the mutually harmful cycle will ever come to an end.

Taking this new approach requires an agile mind. Otherwise the effort will be like trying to put a patch on a surface that isn't sticky— the patch will just fall off. But in order to have mental agility, we must first want to use our minds in new ways. We must seek out whatever qualities it takes to be patient rather than continue with our habitual reactions.

So first you should check yourself and determine if this is something you really want to do. Would you rather apply unconventional thinking that goes against the flow of your habitual ruts, or would you prefer to simply get angry? If you see stronger reasons to get angry than to apply these teachings, then you should get angry! If you contemplate the pros and cons and decide that aggression would serve you best, then you should resort to aggression. But if you think that having a peaceful heart would serve you better than aggression, then this kind of unconventional thinking is very helpful.

Either way, we shouldn't think that bodhisattvas are phony people who act well in an outward way but don't really mean it. We shouldn't think that deep down they are as angry as we are—or even worse—and that on top of that they are charlatans. This is not true. Bodhisattvas use these practices because they work to bring peace to the mind. The attitude of bodhicitta works as an antidote to all disturbing emotions. If these methods don't work for us, we should ask ourselves if that is because we are addicted to anger.

To make progress on this bodhisattva path requires tremendous honesty and openness with ourselves. But when we are in pain, it is hard to have such honesty, especially about the cause of the pain. What is the immediate main cause of our pain when we are aggressive? The answer is very simple: it is the aggression itself. That is what directly hurts us. It is like getting burned when you touch a hot stove. The cause of the burn is undeniably the hot stove. To look for a more significant cause not only doesn't make sense, but it also prevents us from learning from the experience and not repeating the mistake over and over. This is a very important and often overlooked understanding.

If we really tune in to how much our own aggression hurts us, it will be harder to justify getting angry. After all, it is really our own mind and its experience that we are speaking of here. When we recognize this, we will feel compelled to rise up and break our addiction to anger by finding better solutions than meekly letting the emotion overpower us. We will then have a strong incentive to apply the ingenious, unconventional methods practiced by Shantideva and other great exemplars of nonviolence in this world. From this place, our mind will become more and more agile in dealing with difficult situations.

When we see for ourselves how our own aggression causes us so much suffering, we will have a valuable piece of knowledge. We should appreciate this knowledge, for it is a great blessing. Anything that directs us toward taking responsibility for our own mind and emotions is a blessing, whereas the habit of always looking out and blaming someone or something else for our pain is a curse. What makes this habit especially unfortunate is that usually we have no chance of altering the outer circumstances, so we can feel trapped between our outer conditions and our habitual emotional reactions. As Shantideva says in an earlier chapter of his book:

To cover all the earth with sheets of leather—
Where could such amounts of skin be found?
But with the leather soles of just my shoes
It is as though I cover all the earth!

This is the attitude we need to cultivate in order to succeed in our patience practice. Trying to cover the earth with leather—meaning trying to make all our outer conditions smooth and to our liking—is not only frustrating, it is also a complete waste of our precious time.

Shantideva's language—for example, calling himself a "torturer"—may seem to be an expression of self-loathing. But this is not where he's coming from. Getting stuck in the mind-set of "I'm bad" is really just an excuse to avoid doing the honest self-reflection needed to work with our mind and reactions. Self-loathing actually goes hand in hand with blaming others. They feed off each other. First we try to blame others; when we've had enough of that, we turn the blame on ourselves. We go back and forth between these two fruitless methods. This is like the Indian analogy of the elephant bath. On a hot day, an elephant takes a bath in the river to cool down. When it comes out, the elephant wants to get dry, so it rolls around in the dirt. Then it must go back into the river to get the dirt off, and so on.

This kind of effort will never accomplish anything. It is also very tiresome, as we can all attest. I myself am quite fed up with my own tendency to bathe like an elephant. The question of who is to blame is irrelevant. From the standpoint of dependent origination, no one is at fault in the way we conventionally think and fixate on. Things happen in the way they happen due to countless causes and conditions. When we try to isolate one person or one thing to blame, we are confining our vision to an extremely short time span and forgetting about the vast, cyclical, and infinitely complex nature of samsara.

Mature practitioners like Shantideva can look at all aspects of a situation objectively, without needing to defend their past behavior or blame others. Any of our sufferings in the present must come from our own ignorant wrongdoings in the past. That is the law of karma, not a sign of intrinsic badness. All sentient beings, including our-selves, have an enlightened nature even while we are ignorant and wander in samsara. We should learn to identify with the unchanging, skylike nature of our being rather than our transient, smokelike faults and misunderstandings. This will give us the strength and confidence to be able to understand what is happening in our lives. It will enable us to act in a way that will move us further along the path until we fully realize our enlightened nature and bring vast benefit to others.

43
Their weapons and my body—
Both are causes of my torment!
They their weapons, I my body brandished;
Who then is more worthy of my rage?

44
This body—running sore in human form—
Merely touched, it cannot stand the pain!
I'm the one who grasped it in my blind attachment,
Whom should I resent when pain occurs?

The body is one of our most precious resources. The teachings com-pare it to a boat that can take us where we want to go. For the bodhi-sattva, this means crossing the ocean of samsara and reaching the shore of enlightenment. Therefore, we should sustain our bodies ap-propriately, giving them the food, clothing, medicine, and exercise they require.

The body, however, becomes a torment when we become exces-sively attached to it. Then we overreact when faced with even small harms. If we step on a thorn or are touched by a spark of fire, we may fly into a panic. Most of us are also painfully attached to our body image. Our feeling of well-being is powerfully influenced by how we think we look. We go through tremendous hope and fear—about our clothes, our weight, our upcoming haircut. These forms of attachment to the body make us susceptible to anger when anything appears to threaten it. In this way, rather than being a boat for crossing the shore, the body can become more like an anchor that sinks our boat in the depths of samsara.

We suffer from this excessive attachment because we equate our body with our very existence. We do not see the body for what it is—a temporary dwelling place for the mind. Before you were born, you were a disembodied consciousness looking for a home. Through your karmic connection to your parents, your consciousness came together with your mother's egg and father's sperm, and this microscopic physical structure became your home. It remained your home as it developed and grew, and it will continue to serve in this way until this life comes to its inevitable end and your consciousness must move on to another body and another life.

Contemplating the natural, universal cycle of life is one effective method for working with our attachment to the body and the fear that comes with it. If we don't recognize and work with this excessive attachment, we will have a major obstacle to our patience practice. When we are threatened, we will have a one-sided view of what is happening. We will see a problem coming at us from the outside and fixate only on that, while failing to see the greater problem within— the problem of our excessive attachment to the body. From this more balanced perspective, it is overreactive and illogical to get angry only at our outer enemies. This, however, is not an encouragement to get angry at our own mind as well. Shantideva is only pointing out the irony of our irrational thinking by poking holes in the fabric of our beliefs, which we assumed were so solid and real.

Here, as usual, we can inspire ourselves with the examples of the buddhas and bodhisattvas, many of whom are embodied in the great masters of our own time. Because they have gone beyond this excessive attachment to the body through their efforts in study, contemplation, and meditation, they have no reason to defend it from threats. Even were the entire universe to turn upside down, they would have no anxiety about their body. They are living proof that it is possible to overcome even our most primal attachment. As we continue to follow the bodhisattva path, it will become clearer how all phenomena—including this body—are as illusory as rainbows. At that point, we will no longer be provoked to aggression when our body is threatened.

45
We who are like children
Shrink from pain but love its causes.
We hurt ourselves through our misdeeds!
So why should others be the object of our rage?

This stanza is both poetic and truthful. We don't like pain, but we do like to indulge in actions that cause us pain. Anything we do that is based on attachment, anger, jealousy, or arrogance creates negative karma for us. In other words, anything we do based on cherishing or protecting the self—this self that is mere illusion—will eventually bring about our own suffering. Until we learn to work with these emotions or states of mind—especially their excessive, destructive versions—we will inevitably experience pain.

There is no reason to point the finger at some external enemy, blaming the outside world or conditions for our reactions. Here our pain is truly self-inflicted. It is important to recognize this, and as we begin to do so, it is critical to view this recognition with the right attitude. We must not fall prey to any habitual self-grasping and self-loathing. That is not the point of this teaching. The issue at hand is our confusion, and here we are becoming liberated by seeing the truth. So we must take heart and be glad that we finally see. At no time do these teachings encourage us to feel bad. If you find yourself there, reflect and adjust your point of view.

46
And who indeed should I be angry with?
This pain is all my own contriving—

Likewise all the janitors of hell
And all the groves of razor trees!

This is a very profound teaching, which I always try to remember when my world is becoming threatening and I'm starting to feel paranoid. It is said that one can take birth in forests where, instead of leaves, the trees have swords that cut the beings' bodies into little pieces. Such terrifying places exist in samsara, though no creator or powerful being has made them. There is no one to blame for the razor trees, no one for us to be angry with. They only appear due to our own past actions.

Those who are learned in the Buddhist teachings don't become despondent when suffering comes into their lives. They know that everything happens because of karma—that what one gets is what one has given, or as they say, "What goes around, comes around." Our own aggression and the actions that arise from it can plant seeds that ripen into realms of intense suffering. On the other hand, our patience practice can prevent such things from happening because by working with our reactive minds, we can give circumstances enough room to unfold and purify themselves. When we don't react, we don't perpetuate negative actions. That is the starting point of exhausting our negative karma.

If we have a tool like the practice of patience, we have a supreme advantage and can even take great joy in any opportunity to purify our past negative deeds. This perspective is a game changer. We do have great power to influence our future. In the present, however, we may still have to endure the results of much past negativity.

There's a traditional story about a monk named Ravati who was dyeing his robes in a pot when a man came by searching for his stray calf. He asked Ravati what he was doing, and the monk told him. But then the man demanded to see what was in the pot, and when Ravati took off the lid, they both saw meat being boiled. Ravati was then brought to the king, who had him thrown into a pit for stealing the calf. Soon after, the mother cow found the lost calf on her own. The man, feeling remorse, asked the king to release Ravati. But the king got distracted and left the monk in the pit for six months. Finally, a group of Ravati's disciples approached the king, who went to release him. Seeing what poor condition Ravati was in, the king felt terrible. But the monk said, "Don't apologize. This is not what you think. It's my own karma returning to me." Then he told a story about how he had stolen a calf in a past life. When people came to track down the calf, he left it at a hermit's doorstep and ran away, which resulted in the hermit being thrown into a pit. Because of this one action, he had had to endure many forms of suffering, of which this was the last. So, instead of being resentful, Ravati was relieved to have this opportunity to burn up that karma once and for all.

We can learn to adopt a similar perspective when misfortune hits. This is not about being a martyr, but about having a precise and wakeful mind armed with the practice of patience. We should try this approach with small misfortunes and slowly build our strength of patience and profound acceptance of our karma. It is worth mentioning again that this is an inner practice of the mind, heart, and emotions. Don't confuse the context of this practice and jump to the conclusion that Shantideva is recommending we let people walk all over us. In life, when we are off the meditation cushion, we must all abide and expect others to abide by the laws of the land and to respect one another's boundaries.

The Buddha's very first teaching, the first of the Four Noble Truths, is that all beings in samsara go through continual suffering. However, one of the great strengths of the Buddha's teachings is that they don't leave us at a loss about what to do with our suffering. We can always find a way to make use of it on the bodhisattva path. We can be like Gelongma Palmo, a nun who was poisoned by a *naga*—a powerful serpent spirit—and then became sick with leprosy. In her pain and isolation, she contemplated the sufferings of all sentient beings who similarly have to experience the fruits of their karma. As a result, she became devoted to Avalokiteshvara, the bodhisattva of compassion. She was able to meet him and speak to him in person, and from there she became realized and benefited many beings. There are many stories like this in both the past and the present.

These days, however, it is harder for people to trust in the law of karma. Even though karma is taught all the time and we can find many clear examples of how it plays out just as the teachings say, we tend to lack faith and understanding. But lack of faith and understanding is not a static condition. It's not as though we are or are not born with these qualities and that is how it will remain forever. Like any other positive quality of mind—patience is a good example—we can choose to cultivate them. If we see the benefits of doing so, we can start by simply being open to the possibility of karma and then being curious to know more.

Some people resist believing in karma because they think it means blaming victims for their misfortune. This is a misunderstanding. After Hurricane Katrina hit Louisiana in 2005, Larry King interviewed His Holiness the Dalai Lama. "How do you explain how this could happen to good people?" he asked him. "Doesn't it make you question your faith?" His Holiness tried to explain how, from the Buddhist point of view, everything happens because of karma, but King had trouble hearing him. When misfortune happens, it can be hard, on top of that, to hear someone telling you it's because of your karma. But other explanations make less sense and are equally hard to hear. How does it help to think of a misfortune as God's will? Why would God do something so unkind to his own creation? How does it help to think of it as random? If things happened randomly—in other words, without a cause—then there would be complete chaos, and we would always be on edge. These explanations leave one feeling helpless and without any way ahead.

Conviction in the law of karma—along with deeply accepting our own karma—can bring a tremendous sense of relief and open up a whole new avenue to work with the mind in difficult situations without feeling victimized and powerless. It releases us from the feeling that we are struggling helplessly against mysterious forces that bring us suffering. We feel more at ease with whatever happens to us and have a better sense of how to navigate our lives going forward. This enables us to forgive and move on. Since positive karma is based on altruism and negative karma is based on self-centered mind, we have a simple formula for how to go from year to year and from life to life with increasing joy, peace, and confidence.

Confidence and faith in karma also strengthens our motivation to work hard on the path to enlightenment. Milarepa, the most renowned yogin in the history of Tibet, demonstrated such extraordinary devotion to his practice that some of his disciples thought he must have come into this world as the emanation of a buddha. Though he appreciated this mark of their respect, he told them that they were completely mistaken. When he was young, to carry out his mother's vengeful wishes, he had killed thirty-five people at a wedding feast by using black magic to make the house collapse. It was his subsequent fear of the karmic repercussions of this action that later drove him to practice with such determination and endure such extreme hardships for the sake of realizing the dharma. He told his disciples that if they had an equally strong conviction in karma, the natural law of cause and effect, they would not have much trouble accomplishing what he had.

The encouragement to understand and develop faith in karma, or cause and effect, is not an encouragement to abandon the reasoning mind. Logic and reasoning are important components of the Buddhist path and only support the understanding of karma. The great masters such as Nagarjuna and Shantideva had intellects far more sophisticated than our own. Instead of following the Buddha's teachings blindly, they followed his advice to "examine my teachings the way a goldsmith examines gold." Their teachings are not founded on a naive bias toward the dharma. But at the same time, they understood that reasoning alone is not enough.

We don't always have the means to figure everything out, especially when it comes to karma and past and future lives. To complement our logical mind, we must be able to trust. Otherwise we will just go from one intellectual insight to another, enjoying small bursts of "Yeah! Yeah!" as we break through minor places of confusion but not really getting anywhere in the long run. This way of studying the dharma won't help us get free of our clinging to a self, which is the root cause of all our pain. Therefore, it is not enough to liberate us from samsara.

In difficult times, the mind tends to spin out, grasping for explanations and looking for someone or something to blame in order to offload our pain. This kind of mental ordeal only compounds our suffering. What we really need is a place for the mind to rest. Understanding karma and conviction in its natural law provides us with such a place. It allows us to accept our conditions, which gives us room in our minds and hearts to continue on our path without being weighed down with discouragement or despair.

47
Those who harm me rise against me—
It's my karma that has summoned them.
And if through this, these beings go to hell,
Is it not I who bring their ruin?

Because we have wronged beings in the past, things have naturally come around for them to wrong us in the present. But by harming us now, they are sowing seeds for their own future pain. Therefore, instead of being angry with them, why not have compassion?

This may seem like a big stretch, especially in the middle of a heated or painful situation. But once things have cooled down, if you can return to the situation in your mind and reflect on this verse, it can help you gain perspective.

48
Because of them, and through my patience,
All my many sins are cleansed and purified.
But they will be the ones who, thanks to me,
Will have the long-drawn agonies of hell.

Again, Shantideva uses unconventional thinking. When someone harms us, we tend to feel like a victim, or at least that we have been wronged, but from the standpoint he presents here, we are benefiting from the action. By practicing patience in the face of provocation, our karma is burned up, and we grow in mental strength and tolerance. The merit of this practice will elevate us in this life and in lives to come. On the other hand, those who harm us, coming back to repay us for past harms, are ensuring their own future suffering.

Bodhisattvas who think in this way feel genuine compassion for those who do them harm. We may be skeptical and say, "How could someone be so pure and clean? This seems like wishful thinking. Nobody could really do that. It sounds only theoretical." But bodhisattvas are not phonies. They have developed deep compassion in their hearts through repeatedly contemplating the sufferings of others. They have diligently practiced imagining themselves in others' shoes. As a result, they fully appreciate the pain of feeling angry, the pain of intending to harm someone else, the pain of acting with aggression, and the pain of experiencing the consequences. This understanding enables bodhisattvas to sympathize with those who do harm, even when they themselves are the object of that harm. They have also gone beyond their clinging to a self, which enables them to go through any experience without feeling personally threatened. This gives them tremendous strength to dwell in a state of present, peaceful compassion rather than fear or resentment.

We can train our own minds to be as strong and sane as the mind of a bodhisattva. Again, this is a realistic possibility, not just a theoretical idea. We have to remember that at some point in their existence, every bodhisattva was even more confused and vulnerable than we are now. If they could rise from that state and gradually achieve the ability to feel deep compassion for those who harm them, then so can we.

There is no reason to sabotage your self-confidence by thinking, *Maybe it's possible for others to develop compassion and wisdom, but it's not possible for me. I'm a horrible practitioner, a total disappoint-*

ment to myself and my teachers. If this is your mind-set, ask yourself sincerely why it's not possible for you. What makes you so different? You eat food and drink water just like everybody else. You go to the bathroom in the same way. You are capable of doing what other human beings can do. You are well educated—you know how to read, to think, to learn. You even have access to all the teachings and practices that have brought the bodhisattvas to where they are now. So in what way are you lacking?

If you think your neuroses are worse than those of others, that is just your assumption. When they started out on the path, the buddhas and bodhisattvas had all the same neuroses you do now. That is why there are so many teachings to address and work with our minds. The Buddha's teachings work because essentially we all have the same makeup of mind, the same types of thoughts, emotions, habits, reactions, and ignorance.

With these reflections in mind, we should ask ourselves whether we are just making excuses because we simply don't want to take charge of our mind and maybe don't want to change yet. In a later chapter, Shantideva speaks of self-deprecation as one of the most harmful forms of laziness. Instead he encourages us to have a can-do attitude. The dharma has powerful antidotes against anger, fear, self-doubt, and every other disturbing emotion and state of mind. With complete confidence in his ability to apply these proven methods, he says, "I'll not surrender to the host of the afflictions, but like a lion I will stand amid a crowd of foxes."

From such a position of strength, bodhisattvas can genuinely be more concerned about others than themselves. This is the bodhisattva's real heart. What freedom it is to have such a heart!

49
Therefore I am their tormentor!
Therefore it is they who bring me benefit!
Thus with what perversity, pernicious mind,
Will you be angry with your enemies?

50

If a patient quality of mind is mine,
I shall avoid the pains of hell.
But though indeed I save myself,
What of my foes? What fate's in store for them?

If, as the previous verse suggests, we are causing those who wrong us to suffer in the future, aren't we behaving in the opposite way to the bodhisattvas? Isn't there a way to avoid causing them harm?

Yes, this is something to think about with concern. But at the same time, what can we do about someone else's mind? We can't go into it and remove their hostility toward us, and we can't stop the aggressive speech and actions that naturally arise from an angry mind. We would if we could, but such a thing is not possible. Most of the time, there's not much we can do other than feel compassion and say prayers on their behalf.

We may also wonder about generating negative karma for ourselves because of the harm we are doing to them. Won't this come back to haunt us in the future? The answer is no, this is not something we need to worry about because the most important factor in karma is our intention. If we have no intention to harm those who attack us, if we do not hope for or rejoice in the karmic consequences of their actions, if instead we only wish them to be happy and free from suffering, then we are only generating positive karma for ourselves. Our concern for these people comes from the tsewa in our hearts. Thoughts and actions that arise from tsewa accumulate merit, not negative karma. If we dedicate this merit on their behalf, it will benefit them in the long run. Perhaps in a future life, when we have made more progress as bodhisattvas, we may find ourselves in a better position to benefit them directly, say by sharing the dharma with them.

51

If I repay them harm for harm,
Indeed they'll not be saved thereby.

My conduct will in turn be marred,
Austerity of patience brought to nothing.

If you don't protect your mind in these situations by practicing patience, then both parties will be brought down. The person who harms you is already generating negative karma by acting out of aggression. You can't protect them from that because you can't control someone else. But with mindfulness and introspection, you can control yourself. If instead you react and retaliate, you will not only harm yourself, you will also provoke the next round of anger in the other person, which will have further consequences, and so on.

In his commentary *The Nectar of Manjushri's Speech*, Kunzang Pelden highlights four difficult tasks that we have to perform in order to protect and further enhance our patience. These are: not to argue back when someone argues with you; not to return anger with anger; not to strike back when someone strikes you; and not to say hurtful things and press on someone's sore spots when they do those things to you. When we face any of these challenging situations, we have an opportunity to increase our resilience. If instead we give in to anger every time, we will never grow or strengthen our patience practice, and we will have a hard time protecting our bodhicitta.

The bodhisattva path has four stages. In the beginning stage, we don't know how to protect ourselves or others. At the second stage, we gain the ability to protect ourselves. For example, when provoked, we know how to protect our mind with patience. This is the stage we are working with right now. We are getting better at protecting our own mind from succumbing to our habitual ruts and harmful reactiveness, but we can do little to protect the minds of others.

At the third stage, when our bodhicitta has grown to the point where we care more for others than for ourselves, the situation will be somewhat reversed. We will then be better at protecting others than ourselves. In a previous life, the Buddha was a sea captain who was traveling across the ocean with five hundred merchants. They encountered a pirate named Black Spearman, who threatened to kill all the merchants. Realizing that such an act would cause the pirate to suffer a dreadful series of future lives, the captain killed him out of compassion. He understood the grave consequences of killing but risked his own future to spare Black Spearman the future suffering that would result from his intention to kill. Because this act was motivated by genuine compassion, free of self-interest, the captain actually gained immense merit.

When we reach the final stage, we will be like the Buddha himself. We will have the wisdom and skillful means to protect both others and ourselves. An illustration of this is the story of Ajatashatru, a prince who killed his father. The Buddha was able to help him purify his deeds and guide him to the extent that Ajatashatru became the Buddha's most important patron and eventually a great bodhisattva.

SIX

Practicing Patience When We Are Treated with Contempt

52

Because the mind is bodiless
It cannot be destroyed by anyone.
Because of mind's attachment to the body,
This body is oppressed by pain.

53

Scorn and hostile words,
And comments that I do not like to hear—
My body is not harmed by them.
What reason do you have, O mind, for your resentment?

54

The enmity that others show me,
Since in this or future lives
It cannot actually devour me,
Why should I be so averse to it?

The forty stanzas before this section (12 through 51) have focused on our aversion to any kind of physical, emotional, or mental pain. This fear of pain is one of the eight worldly concerns that create yi midewe ze—food that disturbs our mind. Now, beginning with verse 52, Shantideva goes into the other aversions that are part of our eight worldly concerns. First, he explains how to practice patience when people treat us with contempt.

Most of us are fortunate not to experience much physical violence in our personal lives. Unless we are in an abusive relationship, it is rare for other people to hurt our bodies. It is also uncommon for intruders to come into our homes and take our possessions by force. For most of us, the violence we experience comes in the form of words. People insult each other, slander each other, spread rumors, insinuate, and undermine friendships and relationships with their divisive speech. We get into "You said this" and "You said that," which becomes a rapidly escalating war of words and misunderstandings. These verbal assaults create so much of the suffering in our world.

Here Shantideva asks us to examine the following: When you are on the receiving end of unpleasant words and rumors, where do you get hurt? Is it in your mind or in your body? If you say it's your mind, then look into what that "mind" is. Does your mind have a shape, form, color, location, or any other tangible quality? Is there anything at all that you can pinpoint as "mind"? If you do this investigation and can't find anything, then what is being harmed? How could something without any substance be touched by words? How could something completely unfindable be hurt in any way?

On the other hand, do the words that hurt you inflict pain on your body? Obviously they don't. Words themselves have no substance. They are not like knives or bullets. Someone calling you a name or slandering you won't move a single hair on your body. You may feel strong sensations in your chest, throat, or head, but are these caused by the words or your reactions in your own mind? These sensations, too, are elusive. When we try to characterize them, we find they are hard to pin down.

There is no way for words to hurt the mind or body, yet we are frequently hurt by others' speech. That is because we are in a state of misunderstanding. Because of our mistaken belief in an intrinsic self, we have many attachments that make us vulnerable. We are painfully attached to our images and ideas about this fictitious self—attached to who we think we are and how we would like to see ourselves. Trying to protect and preserve these ideas is the true cause of why we get hurt. Buddhas and bodhisattvas who have gone beyond self-clinging don't have these vulnerabilities, so they are not bothered by any negative words about themselves. The remedy here is not to focus on the insults or storylines, but to look within and confront this sense of self and its attachments. Going directly to the root of the pain in this way will free us more than tracking who said what and why. We will thus become less vulnerable to words, which in reality have no ability to harm us.

Words are simply sounds, echoes. They only hurt us when our minds hold on to the idea that they are real and are directed toward us with intent to harm. Here it can be helpful to imagine that you are an actor in a play. Another actor is verbally abusing you, shouting all kinds of vulgar words in your face. But you are playing a person who easily shrugs off insults, who doesn't take them seriously at all. Even if your character reacts with anger, you the actor don't feel angry. You're not thinking the other actor intended to treat you with contempt. Because everything is in the context of the play, none of the actions and emotions are real, so no one feels hurt or confused. This is something to contemplate.

The words we hear in life and the words we hear in a play could be identical. They could be delivered at the same volume and with the same intonation. But in our day-to-day lives, we generally hold on to all the parts of the scenario as real: the words are real, the insulter is real, their intention to harm us is real, and we ourselves are real. An actor on a stage—even one who has never meditated or received any dharma teachings—knows that all of these are mere illusions. The only difference between the two situations is what the mind believes. If we train ourselves to see the illusory nature of scorn and contempt, we will have no fear of them. Instead of hurting us in this life or the next, they will promote our well-being by giving us opportunities to perfect our patience. Therefore, we can see them as a service we have received without our even having to ask.

55
Perhaps I turn from it because
It hinders me from having what I want.
But all my property I'll leave behind,
While sins will keep me steady company.

We may think, *I understand this reasoning about why words can't harm my body or mind. But they do affect me in other ways. If my reputation is ruined, that will affect my livelihood and prosperity. Good things will stop coming into my life. Therefore, I am justified in getting angry.* In response, Shantideva asks us to consider whether it is worth trying to protect ourselves from slander and so on by causing ourselves far greater harm—the karmic consequences, in this and future lives, of acting out with aggression.

How much do our standing in life and material prosperity really benefit us? Our excessive attachment to these things inevitably leads us to pile up many harmful thoughts and actions. They make our minds vulnerable to becoming overreactive. If we find ourselves lashing out so much because our livelihood and possessions are threatened, we should take a step back and ask ourselves, *Is this really good for me? Is my highly coveted job really benefiting me, or is it making me act like a monster? Is my wealth helping me, or am I just becoming more stingy and self-centered? Is my status making me defensive, arrogant, and more isolated?* It is important to practice honest self-reflection around these questions.

We may take for granted the desirable nature of wealth, power, and status. But even if we've worked all our lives for such things, it is now time to reexamine them from a distance. We must try to have some perspective on how they actually serve our higher aspirations. Do they serve us, or do they enslave us? If you have wealth, you don't want to be a servant to that wealth. You want to be its master so you can use it to benefit yourself and others. If you have a good position, you want to use it for a good purpose rather than becoming its slave. But we can only be masters of our livelihood, our wealth, our possessions, and our station in life by first working with our ingrained attachments to them.

56

Better far for me to die today,
Than live a long and evil life.
However long the days of those like me,
The pain of dying will be all the same.

It is important to sustain ourselves through this life, but at the same time we must consider the bigger picture. This life is just one life in an infinite continuum. Our mind has been here long before our present body and will continue long after this body is gone. No matter how much we cherish and protect this present life, in a relatively short time—a matter of decades at most—it will come to an end. For someone like Shantideva, whose mind is set on becoming liberated from samsara and attaining enlightenment for the benefit of all beings, it is better to live a shorter life than to keep sustaining himself through accumulating negativity.

In his *Garland of Jewels*, the master Nagarjuna lists five "poisonous" ways in which people try to gain material support or possessions for themselves. The first is giving gifts in the hope of getting bigger gifts in return. The second is praising an object in such a way that the other person feels obliged to give it to you. The third way is hinting that you are poor and need something the other person has. Fourth is using your position or power to put pressure on others so they feel compelled to give you what you want. Finally, there is acting as if you're worthy of receiving gifts because of your good qualities. For example, you cunningly pretend to be an altruistic person or a great practitioner.

When we behave in any of these sneaky ways, our mind becomes immersed in a painful state of covetousness. We start to see the world as our tangerine. The purpose of our precious human life is reduced to squeezing that tangerine, trying to extract as much juice as possible.

But no matter how much juice we squeeze, it is never enough. Instead of alleviating our acute sense of lack, this behavior only makes it worse.

Nagarjuna's teachings were mainly directed at monastics, but it is easy to see how these poisonous forms of conduct are used in today's business world. The Buddha taught that generosity is the only reliable cause of wealth. But the profit-oriented, business state of mind is the complete opposite of what we try to cultivate through the practice of generosity. Instead of bringing a feeling of richness into our lives, these tricky types of behavior really bring about a feeling of deep dissatisfaction. No matter how much you have at your disposal, your mind is always fixated on more profits. If a day goes by without any progress in your financial sphere, you feel agitated. Even though you can afford to do so, you don't want to spend even one whole day in leisure. When you go on vacation, you take all your devices with you to keep up with the business. Thus, relaxation becomes impossible. And if you go through life this way, the habit of juicing the world keeps getting worse. If this pattern continues, even if you maintain and increase your wealth in this life, the most likely result will be poverty in your next one.

Shantideva had such integrity as a bodhisattva that he could genuinely prefer an early death over following a dismal path toward karmic ruin. But in this stanza, he is also making a strong statement to illustrate his point. In reality, our choice is not so stark: we are not forced to choose between dying today and having a deceitful livelihood. There are many ways for us to earn a sufficient living through honest labor. But if we are working nonstop just for a chance to become CEO, we should think deeply about the long-term results, especially regarding our path to enlightenment. Having done so, we may then conclude that it would be better to go into a different line of work, perhaps as a schoolteacher, bus driver, or social worker.

57
One man dreams he lives a hundred years
Of happiness, but then he wakes.

Another dreams an instant's joy,
But then he likewise wakes.

58
And when they wake, the happiness of both
Is finished, never to return.
Likewise, when the hour of death comes round,
Our lives are over, whether brief or long.

59
Though we be rich in worldly goods,
Delighting in our wealth for many years,
Despoiled and stripped as though by thieves,
We must go naked and with empty hands.

Whether life is long or short, when it's over, it's over. At that point, it won't matter how many possessions and pleasurable experiences we have or haven't had. It is just like having a dream. Whether the dream is long or short, pleasant or painful, it vanishes completely as soon as we wake up. We can't take any of it with us.

At first glance, thinking along these lines may seem sad and depressing, but when done with a positive attitude, it makes our minds lighter and more cheerful. See if this isn't so yourself. The most positive attitude we can have is bodhicitta, the mind-set of awakening, which carries with it the magnificent vision of attaining enlightenment over lifetimes for the benefit of others. From this point of view, what is really sad and depressing is how deeply attached we are to the illusory phenomena of samsara. Because of our attachments, we do so many harmful things and have to face so many painful consequences. In most cases, we're even aware that our attachments don't serve us, yet our bondage to them is too overpowering.

The only way to free ourselves from this bondage is by letting go, but letting go is not as simple as it sounds. It requires critical intelligence and self-reflection to identify the confusion at the root of our bondage. That is why contemplations such as those in these stanzas are so important. They are a good example of one of Shantideva's specialties—having a straight talk with himself. If we really want to be free of our bondage to attachment, aggression, and other painful states, we would be wise to follow Shantideva's lead.

We can talk with ourselves in this way: *My life will come to an end. When I'm on my deathbed, which will happen sooner than I think, everything I have gathered and accomplished will be in the past. What will matter then is how well I can face my death and my fear of the unknown next world. For this the most important factor is the state of my heart, specifically my tsewa and bodhicitta. So why should I be driven by all these attachments to temporary things? Why go through so much anxiety and stress, and why run myself into the ground while committing so many actions that harm myself and others along the way?*

This kind of straight talk won't immediately free us from our excessive attachments, but it should weaken the blind intensity of our drives. We tend to go around with minds full of anxiety about meeting our needs and fulfilling our desires. Thinking about impermanence and death loosens the grip these things have on us. It gives us space from our anxiety and perspective on our lives.

It's not that we don't strive to care for ourselves and others in a reasonable way. Fulfilling our basic human needs for nourishment, safety, and love with positive regard for ourselves is not a problem. This teaching addresses the excessive drive that can take over our lives when we leave our tendencies unchecked. Contemplating death with these intentions in mind brings us to a more open-hearted state. Then, whether or not our attachments are fulfilled, we feel that we have lightened our load. This is a great kindness to our mind.

60

Perhaps we'll claim that by our wealth we live,
And living, gather merit, dissipating evil.
But if we are aggressive for the sake of profit,
Won't our gains be evil, all our merits lost?

61

And if the aim for which we live
Is thereby wasted and undone,
What use is there in living thus,
When evil is the only consequence?

You might think it's important to accumulate wealth so you can do positive things. You could have ideas about building a temple and filling it with blessed statues, building a hospital or a school, or being very generous to the poor. Through these activities, you hope to accumulate tremendous merit, which you will then dedicate to becoming enlightened for the sake of all sentient beings. Having these generous visions in your mind, wouldn't you be justified in using aggression to protect your wealth?

Shantideva says that this way of thinking is foolish. If you're living your life for merit, there is no better way to accumulate and protect that merit than by practicing patience. When you get angry, even if you have some so-called justification, you destroy much of the merit you have accumulated. Furthermore, the drive for wealth can bring you all sorts of suffering: jealousy, insecurity, one-upmanship, fear, disappointment. Gathering wealth more often leads to increased stinginess than increased generosity. Instead of doing helpful things for others or even using the money for ourselves, we may well turn into misers, mere guardians of our wealth. Can you be sure that you won't end up like so many before you have?

So why go to so much trouble to amass wealth? If wealth comes to you naturally because of your past generosity, then you can appreciate it and do something positive with it. On the other hand, if your past negative deeds are now resulting in limited resources or loss of your wealth, you have the opportunity to purify your karma through the practice of patience. As long as you can make ends meet, there is no particular need for great wealth to progress on the spiritual path and be a genuinely happy person. There are plenty of other ways to gather merit and benefit others. So why not learn to be satisfied with a simpler, more peaceful life—a life of little needs and much contentment? Why not focus on opening your heart and gathering tsewa, a wealth far more fulfilling, enriching, and joyful than anything that can be gained in the material world?

62

And if, when people slander us,
We claim our anger is because they injure others,
How is it we do not resent
Their slander when it's aimed at someone else?

63

And if we bear with this antipathy
Because it's due to other factors,
Why are we impatient when they slander us?
Defilement, after all, has been the cause of it.

Shantideva reveals yet another angle on the situation. When someone slanders us, their words often influence other people to have unpleasant thoughts about us as well. We may feel concerned about these people who have been influenced because of the negativities that will surely accumulate in their minds. Because their own thoughts will harm them, out of compassion it seems we should do anything we can to prevent the slander from happening. The fact that we are on the bodhisattva path may make the matter feel even more urgent to us because we have heard about the karmic consequences of thinking badly of bodhisattvas. According to this somewhat presumptuous reasoning, doesn't it make sense to use aggression—only if necessary—to stop the slanderer? Doesn't it at least make sense to feel anger about the harm being done to others?

Although there is something to this logic, it falls short because it is one-sided. Would we think and act in the same way if the slander were aimed at somebody else, even a genuine bodhisattva who is far more realized than we are? In that situation, we'd be more likely to think, *I have no control over other people's feelings and perceptions. They have their own karmic connections, which I can't influence. Why is it my business anyway? I can't help it if people have their likes and dislikes.* If that is our reasoning, Shantideva asks us why it doesn't apply when the slander is about us. He is pointing out the inconsistency in our thinking.

Shantideva's broader point is that anger is illogical. We can make up convincing arguments—convincing, at least, to ourselves—but when they are probed, it is easy to see that they make no sense. The sharpness of anger often makes us believe that we are thinking clearly and are right, but that is an illusion. Anger does not improve the mind in any way. It is a weakness, not a strength. Just like excessive attachment and all the other states of mind and emotions based on a mistaken belief in an intrinsic self, anger blinds us and pushes us toward self-destructive behavior.

Our anger can be so illogical that when we are in its grip, we can hardly distinguish between our closest loved ones and those who are really against us. When we lose our temper with our loved ones, our fury and desire to say or do something hurtful can be so strong it's as if we are confronting our worst enemy. We can completely forget that our spouse, parent, or child is our ally in life. This is a person who generally wants us to be happy and free from pain. Yet we are so deranged by anger that we completely lose sight of reality. However, if there is someone who really doesn't like us, who may be an actual threat to our well-being, we often don't want to face them at all. We do everything we can to avoid confrontation. This avoidance is mostly a good thing. It has intelligence behind it. But there is also an element of cowardice.

With your loved ones, you may feel emboldened to lash out because you assume they will stick around. No matter how badly you lose your temper, your mother will still be your mother, your child will still be your child. It feels relatively safe to get angry with them. But a stranger won't accept your aggression in the same way. Your boss will probably fire you. So when you get angry at your loved ones, it's as if you are taking advantage of that bond and that closeness. You are also taking that connection and that person's love for granted. This behavior is ironic and unfortunate. Toward the very people for whom we should have the most care and the most supportive connection, we often allow ourselves to behave the worst. My mother would often warn me against such behavior by saying, "Don't be like a stomach, smooth on the outside but rough on the inside."

The teachings on bodhicitta emphasize the equality of all sentient beings. We are all identical in our constant desire to have happiness and freedom from suffering, and we all have the potential to fulfill that desire completely by attaining enlightenment. This is one of the key principles of the bodhisattva path. At the same time, we have much more contact with the people who are closest to us and much more opportunity to be triggered emotionally. Therefore, we need to make a special point of practicing patience with our loved ones. Otherwise, we could easily fool ourselves into thinking that we are doing well because of how we behave with strangers or even enemies.

If our habit is to save our irritations and aggression to let loose on those who are nearest, then people will learn not to get close to us. Our relationships will be limited to people who have enough physical and emotional distance for both parties to feel safe. We will be "protected" from situations where we rub skins with others and where our emotions come up against others' emotions. In other words, we will be protected from the direct exposure of our inner weaknesses. But we will also become more and more isolated. Instead of having depth, our relationships will be limited to "Hi," "Bye," and maybe talking about the weather. This lifestyle may be fine if you are a hermit and your aim is to be solitary. But we are not hermits. His Holiness the Dalai Lama likes to say that we are "social animals." We need and depend on friends, family, and community for all aspects of our well-being. That is a fact of human life. So we need to work on our patience toward those we spend the most time with instead of turning them into objects of our irritation and aggression.

If you have twenty opportunities in a day to lose your temper, and you only get irritated fifteen times, that is a big accomplishment for that day. If you then manage to reduce the number to ten times, that is a further accomplishment. You won't be able to get the number down to zero immediately, and there is no pressure to do so. But as your patience practice gains strength and your irritation slowly decreases, leaving greater and greater peace in your heart, you will feel more and more connected to others. If you succeed in doing this with the people in your immediate proximity, then you will be able to do it with everyone you meet. This will give you a feeling of tremendous stability in the world. You should acknowledge this kind of progress in yourself and feel joyful and encouraged.

If we don't practice patience—especially with those closest to us— we will feel the opposite of stability, which is a deep shakiness in the presence of others. That shakiness comes from not trusting our own mind. How can we trust our mind when it is so volatile, when it can so quickly become consumed by aggression and cause harm to ourselves and those closest to us? How can we feel any confidence when our mind is so unreliable?

Cultivating patience is one of the best ways to increase our confidence in ourselves. But in order to cultivate patience, we need to begin with some confidence in the teachings and practices. This confidence can come from examining what Shantideva says and being convinced by the reasoning behind it. Shantideva devotes much of this text to laying out logical arguments. By studying and contemplating his reasoning—such as the reasoning he uses in these verses about slander—our conviction in the validity of the teachings will grow. That will give us the conviction that we must do our best to practice patience in all situations. That conviction, in turn, will help us have the confidence and stability to pursue the bodhisattva path to the very end.

SEVEN

How Should We React When Our Loved Ones Are Mistreated?

64
Even those who vilify and undermine
The Sacred Doctrine, images, and stūpas
Are not proper objects of our anger.
Buddhas are themselves untouched thereby.

Now we move into the verses on cultivating patience toward those who abuse the people we care about. This stanza extends the category to include the dharma and all that is associated with it. From the Buddhist point of view, there is no need for religious wars. If someone disparages the dharma or harms a temple, statue, or venerated text, our first priority is to protect our own mind. Instead of aggression, we should generate compassion, knowing that this action will surely result in painful karmic consequences. From there, we might try to persuade the person not to engage in such destructive behavior or even prevent them physically, but if we don't succeed, we should do our best to refrain from getting angry.

Books, statues, and other physical objects can be damaged, but their essence is beyond harm. The essence of the dharma is the enlightened mind, which is the true nature of the buddhas, the bodhisattvas, and all sentient beings as well. The enlightened mind is beyond the need of our protection. Our aggression can do nothing positive for the dharma. If we get angry in these situations, that is a sign of our attachment and short-sightedness. Instead, we should take the opportunity to meet such circumstances with the practice of patience. This will bring us closer to realizing our own enlightened nature and being able to benefit the wrongdoer in the future.

65

And even if our teachers, relatives, and friends
Are now the object of aggression,
All derives from factors, as we have explained.
This we should perceive and curb our wrath.

If we see our spiritual teachers, family members, or friends being harmed, again we should do our best to refrain from lashing out in anger. But we should be clear: patience is not the same thing as being passive. If we can stop the harm without resorting to aggression, then of course we should. The power of nonviolence to bring about positive change is much greater than the power of anger, as can be seen from the examples of people such as Martin Luther King, Jr. But even if we can't stop harm from being done, we should reflect on how everything happens due to causes and conditions.

None of us can prevent disturbing emotions from arising in our own minds. But what defines us as practitioners of patience is what we do with those emotions when they arise. Ordinarily, once aggression takes hold, it is often difficult not to act out in some way, especially if there is an unchecked habit to do so. The aggressor is not in control. Keeping this in mind will make it easier for us not to exacerbate the situation by adding our own aggression. Instead we should do our best to practice patience.

66

Beings suffer injury alike
From lifeless things as well as living beings.

So why be angry only with the latter?
Rather let us simply bear with harm.

An earthquake can destroy a beautiful temple, but we don't get angry at the earthquake. A fire can injure a dear friend or ravage our home, but we don't get angry at the fire. The reason we don't get angry is that we know these things are not operating through will. We understand that they have no autonomy. Since that understanding effectively curbs our anger, we should apply it to people as well, for people also have no autonomy when blinded by states of mind and emotions that are based on ignorance and confusion.

67
Some do evil things because of ignorance,
Some respond with anger, being ignorant.
Which of them is faultless in such acts?
To whom shall error be ascribed?

68
Instead, why did they act in times gone by
That they are now so harmed at others' hands?
Since everything depends on karma,
Why should I be angry at such things?

If someone wrongs you out of ignorance and you get angry, also out of ignorance, then both of you are under the influence of ignorance. Who can say which of you is better? Even if you think of yourself as a practitioner of the bodhisattva's way of life, at this moment you are not doing any such practice. So how are you different from any ordinary person reacting in an ordinary way?

When one person harms another, it is a case of both parties' karmic circumstances coming together and clashing or playing out. For both people, the seeds for this event were sown sometime in the past, and now both are experiencing the result. Keeping this in mind, we shouldn't focus only on the one who commits the present harm, as if they are solely responsible for the situation. That will only lead to more aggression and further perpetuation of the cycle of causing and receiving harm. As it is said, "An eye for an eye leaves the whole world blind." On the contrary, practitioners should take responsibility for their own past actions and use this occasion to consciously purify karmic seeds. This is an opportunity to put an end to the cycle. We should strive to maintain a connection based on love and care with those who harm us rather than perpetuate the samsaric process of an eye for an eye.

When we get angry, we tend to justify and inflame our anger with any number of "good reasons." In this way, we convince ourselves that so-and-so is not a good person or in some way merits our wrath. Thus, we lose sight of the fact that they are just like us in their longing to be happy and free from suffering. And just like us, they are often unable to bring their actions and intentions together. What they do to achieve happiness often brings about the opposite results.

When we overlook this basic equality among all beings, our justifications actually blind us to the fundamental facts of the situation and cause our hearts to close down. Since a peaceful, open heart is the greatest source of our happiness, when we use our reasoning to justify our aggression, we end up harming ourselves. This is the opposite of intelligence.

It's important, however, to understand that maintaining a positive connection with others doesn't mean abandoning or suppressing the discriminative mind. On the contrary, it is often indispensable to use our sharpest intelligence to assess the people around us. How could you go into business with someone if you don't assess their character by using your critical mind? How could you get married and expect years or decades of marriage to go well if you've never looked at your lover with discriminating eyes? How could you decide to follow a spiritual teacher without first following your own intelligence in making that decision?

In these relationships, you need to think clearly about joining your intentions with your actions. If your intention is to work well with somebody, both of you must have certain qualities that make for a harmonious relationship. If you overlook characteristics in yourself and the other person that will make it difficult to work together—and if you don't find ways to communicate and come to a mutual understanding about how to work with these issues on an ongoing basis—then you are not exercising your critical intelligence.

I've found that in the West, many people have a neurotic relationship with their critical mind. On one hand, they are afraid that being critical means being judgmental, which is a quality they understandably don't want to have. On the other hand, they can be unreasonably critical about people and things they know hardly anything about—even total strangers, such as a person they interact with in a supermarket aisle. This kind of criticism is not the critical intelligence I am referring to. It arises from sheer habit and carelessness. It is a result of not being aware of how judgmental thoughts usually lead to disturbing states of mind and emotions, which hinder us from being fully open to others.

We can learn to be critical without being judgmental or unreasonable—and also without whitewashing things because we can't bear to look at what's happening in our minds or with others around us. Parents have to do this with their children. Otherwise, it's impossible to shape a child's character in a positive way. But in recognizing and working with their children's shortcomings, parents don't lose any of their care and compassion. They may get angry from time to time, but their overall attitude toward their children is positive and loving. Good parents can see their child's unhelpful traits without letting that knowledge stain their view of the person as a whole. Similarly, teachers—both spiritual and secular—need to apply critical intelligence without aggression in order to be effective in their roles.

To be critical based on positive effectiveness—as opposed to the eight worldly concerns—is an essential ability for living well in the world. It will become even more important as we progress on the bodhisattva path and our lives become increasingly oriented toward benefiting others. We see this quality in all the great spiritual teachers. Modern-day bodhisattvas such as His Holiness the Dalai Lama don't try to project some sort of saintly vibe. They don't act from the insecurity of having to show others they are good people. They aren't compelled to be passive and suppress their ability to act with discernment.

Yet they always keep an open heart to others, continually flowing with tsewa, as they help positively orient those under their care. We too are capable of developing this combination of good qualities. To do so, we must work on using our intelligence appropriately while at the same time keeping a vigilant eye on any tendency we might have to get lost in self-centeredness or judgmental aggression.

69
This I see and therefore, come what may,
I'll hold fast to the virtuous path
And foster in the hearts of all
An attitude of mutual love.

When someone is in conflict with one of our friends or loved ones, it is natural for us to side with the person we are close to and share in their resentment toward the other. But by doing so, we are likely to add our own aggression to a situation that needs to be pacified. If we want to be truly helpful, we should try to empathize with both parties and, if appropriate, bring them together and encourage harmony and understanding. If there is nothing we can do to help, then it is usually better to stay out of it and instead make prayers on behalf of both parties.

Thinking unrealistically that we can somehow be the savior of the situation will, more often than not, only heighten the confusion and bring about our own frustration. Often the best course of action is to remain open and loving and to wait until others are ready to move forward. This is an opportunity to develop our own patience in wanting to fix a situation.

Wise and skillful action is only possible if we first cultivate a sense of equanimity toward all sentient beings. At the moment, we are blinded and biased by our own attachments and aversions, which are based on our mistaken belief in an intrinsic self. In other words, how we feel about others is largely based on how they relate to us—how they support or threaten that sense of self within us. Any feelings we have toward others that come from this mistaken belief are bound to change over time. Right now, this person is a friend, that person is a blank stranger, and that other person is an adversary. But has it always been this way, and will it always be this way in the future? When we think about it objectively, it becomes clear that our relationships and feelings toward others—and their feelings toward us—are always changing. This becomes even more obvious when we contemplate past and future lifetimes.

The only emotions that never change and are consistently positive are those based on tsewa. The innately tender heart is always present within us, ready to send out its exuberant warmth when impediments such as anger are removed. Therefore, in this verse Shantideva reiterates the importance of keeping our hearts open toward all beings, full of kind and compassionate thoughts and feelings. It can be very tempting to exclude certain beings we don't feel deserve our affection, but we should remember that any exceptions are based on our own self-oriented attitude. On the bodhisattva path, we need to make a special point of developing love and care for those who bother us the most.

70

Now when a building is ablaze
And flames leap out from house to house,
The wise course is to take and fling away
The straw and anything that spreads the fire.

71

And so, in fear that merit might be all consumed,
We should at once cast far away
Our mind's attachments:
Tinder for the fiery flames of hate.

Once I was staying in a hotel in Bhutan, and there was a big fire in the surrounding forest. Instead of panicking, the hotel employees cut down some nearby trees and prevented the fire from getting closer. This is how we should treat our excessive attachments. Knowing that they can swiftly spread the fire of anger and destroy our peace of mind, we should do whatever we can to let go of them.

One example of a dangerous attachment is our wish to look good in front of others by acting out of conventional notions of "nobility." Blinded by such an attachment, we can end up doing foolish and even harmful things, succumbing to pressures from outside that are often not in line with our inner values. In a previous life, the Buddha was a king who practiced great generosity, freely giving away his possessions to anyone who asked for them. When another king asked him for his prized elephant, the Buddha told him he had already given it away. The king threatened to go to war with him over this. The Buddha thought, *I could go to war and defeat this king quite easily, but many people would die and be reborn in lower realms. So it would be better to run away.* That night, he ran away to the forest. He didn't think about appearing cowardly. He didn't try to figure out a way to save face. Instead he simply removed himself from a situation in which he was likely to use aggression and do great harm. There are many other stories of bodhisattvas who similarly took a seemingly dishonorable position from the conventional point of view.

Each of the eight worldly concerns—pleasure and pain, material gain and loss, praise and criticism, renown and defamation—is like a pile of combustible material that can burn us and those around us. Because we live in such a potentially dangerous situation, it is wise to examine our excessive attachments, especially to our loved ones, for those are the attachments that often make us vulnerable to becoming aggressive when they are threatened. Then we should remember the ways we have learned to work with those attachments and eventually let go of them.

Here it is important to contemplate and come to understand the difference between attachment and genuine love. Attachment always has a strong component of self-centeredness, which can be hidden to us, especially if we haven't examined this before. We see the object of our attachment as an extension of ourselves and as a crucial aspect of our own well-being. When we think about "*my* friend," "*my* lover," "*my* child," there is the presence of "me" in the center. If we look carefully, many of our feelings about that person are related to ourselves—how what they are doing will affect us. We are not thinking of the other person so much as an autonomous being. How often do we put ourselves in the shoes of even our dearest ones to imagine what their experience is like? How often do we respond to them from that place? Although we care for their well-being, much of the advice we give is based on what *we* think is best for them. We are always at the center of our relationships.

Then, if someone insults or attacks our dear friend, our anger rises in their defense, and we lash out in ways that help no one. We may think that this defense is honorable and feel good about ourselves, but what is honorable about causing more harm when harm has already been done? What is honorable about favoring attachment and lashing out in aggression instead of extending our love equally toward all beings? From the perspective of equality, we can instead strive to help both sides through their pain and bring them to reconciliation.

Genuine love is not based on an overwhelming presence of "me." Therefore, it doesn't have the potential to lead to aggression. With love that is untainted by attachment, you have more space in your mind to see the whole situation and act more skillfully for the benefit of all. If you hear someone criticize your child, instead of immediately getting offended and lashing out in overwhelming aggression, you have the freedom not to react at once. You can reflect on any of Shantideva's verses, such as his teachings on karma and the interdependence of all things.

It is inevitable that our feelings toward our close circle contain a mixture of love and attachment. In these relationships, we should do our best to weed out the attachment so that the garden of our love can flourish. If we don't tend to a garden and allow weeds to do what comes naturally, they will proliferate and take over. In the same way, our attachments to people, when left unmonitored, will slowly wear us down and cause both people in the relationship to resent each other.

For example, mothers have tremendous love for their children, which is usually accompanied by tremendous attachment. But every mother has to learn to let go starting from early in the child's life, when she must be able to leave her baby with other people. Unless she is able to let go—increasingly so over time—she will not be able to do other important things with her life, and she will also make the child overly dependent. In many cases, parents end up suffocating their children, who thus have a hard time growing up to become confident individuals. This can lead to painful dynamics that never get resolved. I have seen cases like this that go on until the parent is over ninety and the child is over seventy.

The overall point of these verses is that we aspiring bodhi-sattvas need to reflect on the connection between our attachments and other painful emotions and states of mind. Once this is clear, we then need to come up with a plan to address our attachments in the most intelligent and sane way. This includes making sure we don't throw out the baby with the bathwater by reducing our love and warmth. It takes creativity and strength to work with these tricky aspects of mind, but there's always a way as long as we don't give up easily. In some cases, we may need to go through some suffering to move through our attachments, but in the end these experiences will save us and others from much unnecessary pain. The result will be an increasing freedom from aggression and all its miserable karmic consequences.

72

Is it not a happy chance if when, condemned to death,
A man is freed, his hand cut off in ransom for his life?

And is it not a happy chance if now, to escape hell,
I suffer only the misfortunes of the human state?

My family comes from the Kham region of eastern Tibet. In Khampa culture there is the idea that you should express your anger and never shy away from a fight. If you seem passive or subservient, especially when you or your loved ones have been mistreated, then you will get a bad rap. Because I am very familiar with this culture, I know from experience that this attitude doesn't get anyone to a good place.

Many people, not only Khampas, see nonviolence as a weakness. But it is, in fact, a great strength. To be nonviolent, we have to go deep into ourselves and come out with a way to meet the situation with intelligence, appropriateness, and skill. This is based on having the greater vision of bodhicitta, the wish to attain enlightenment for the benefit of all sentient beings. By keeping bodhicitta in the forefront of our mind, we will not be so biased toward "me" and "mine." When bodhisattvas, or their closest loved ones, are wronged, they try to resolve the situation in a way that will be best for both "victim" and "aggressor."

If we fear that our nonviolence will give us a bad rap, we should weigh our options. We could let loose with anger and aggression and get swept away by the momentum, causing destruction in the present and leading to even more painful consequences in the future. Or we could practice patience and risk the scorn of those who misinterpret our behavior as weak. If we reflect on how unpleasant the first alternative is, it will be a great relief to realize we have the second. Shantideva says this is like being taken out to be executed and then having our punishment reduced to losing only a hand. How thankful we would be in that situation! But in reality, the consequences of nonviolence are far better than losing a hand or even getting a bad rap. The great practitioners of nonviolence—people like Mahatma Gandhi, Nelson Mandela, and Tawakkol Karman—do not have the reputation of being cowards. On the contrary, they are almost universally admired as heroes.

73

If even these, my present pains,
Are now beyond my strength to bear,
Why do I not cast off my anger,
Cause of future sorrows in infernal torment?

The resentment we feel when someone mistreats our loved ones may seem almost unbearable. How can we not react with aggression? But Shantideva, understanding that everything is relative, asks us to put things in perspective. If we work wisely with our present pain—say by using it to develop compassion or relating to it like an immunization—it will soon be over, and we will have avoided creating more pain for ourselves and others in the future. But if we react with anger, we will sow seeds for much worse suffering to come. If we weigh the two options objectively, we will obviously choose the lesser pain. Furthermore, if we care so much for our loved ones, we should do everything we can to pacify their anger and discourage them from creating their own negative karma by retaliating.

74

For the sake of gaining all that I desired,
A thousand times I underwent
The tortures of the realms of hell—
Achieving nothing for myself and others.

75

The present aches are nothing to compare with those,
And yet great benefits will come from them.
These troubles that dispel the pain of wanderers—
It's only right that I rejoice in them.

For countless lifetimes, we have tried to gather goods, to take care of our bodies, to be successful in various ways, but no lasting good has come from these efforts. No matter what conventional approach we've tried, we've always remained trapped in samsara. Our attempts to find happiness and joy have involved attachment, aggression, and other self-centered states of mind that create the opposite result—prolonged suffering. Right now, whatever struggles we may be going through, our human experience is about as good as it gets in samsara. If we look beyond our temporary, fortunate circumstances and think about the experience of the vast majority of beings—for example, the countless people who live in dire poverty without enough food to eat or clean water to drink, or the countless animals that live and die on factory farms—it will be obvious that most of our lifetimes have been far more painful than our current existence. If we carelessly allow ourselves to remain in samsara, odds are we will again find ourselves in states of darkness and misery.

At this moment, however, thanks to our excellent karma in meeting the wisdom of sages such as Shantideva, we have a chance to reverse the self-centered way of being that has always been the root of our torment. We can use the suffering in our lives to develop strength, peace, and freedom in our minds, just as the buddhas and bodhisattvas have done before us.

It is said that bodhisattvas from different world systems choose to be born in this world because of its challenging conditions. If we adopt a similar attitude and see our difficulties and adverse circumstances as opportunities, we can grow quickly in the same way as these bodhisattvas.

The outer conditions of our lives are automatically arranged by our own past actions. There is no point in rejecting the ripening of our karma. Furthermore, as already mentioned, there is not usually much we can do about the emotions and mental states that naturally occur in response to outer events. We don't have much choice about what initially arises in our mind streams. But what happens next can be within the realm of our choice. The wisdom of the dharma gives us a chance not to react—physically, verbally, or mentally—in a predictable and habitual manner. By receiving teachings such as Shantideva's and taking time to understand them, contemplate them, apply them, and integrate them into our way of thinking and being, we become more conscious of the workings of our mind and more able to choose how we react.

We create negative karma when we mindlessly indulge in emotions such as anger. The only reason emotions like anger, jealousy, and pride are labeled "negative" is that they are focused on cherishing and protecting ourselves at the expense of others, and the inevitable result of such behavior is pain. The word "negative" is a translation of *digpa* in Tibetan, which literally means "heavy with consequences." In contrast, we create positive karma when we focus on the well-being of others, allowing our innate tsewa to flow naturally and warm up and bring peace to our hearts, our minds, and the world around us.

Karma may seem predestined, but that is only the case if we are unaware of the moment-to-moment experience of the mind. Karma is constantly ripening for us, but how we respond and what we do with what arises is wide open. By practicing mindfulness and self-reflection, we become more conscious of our internal states and more aware of the danger of letting any negativity run free. Only in doing so can we become proficient at transforming our karma from negative to positive. But all of this has to be done without harsh self-judgment. We are much better off when we take joy in our wonderful opportunity to root out the harmful habits of the mind. This process even affects the physical structure of our brains, removing old ruts and creating new pathways where altruism predominates over self-importance. As the mind and its patterns change in these subtle ways, our karma improves, our conditions improve, and we become wiser, more loving, and more adept at benefiting others. The methods for achieving this transformation are contained in these verses by Shantideva.

Such progress is within the reach of all of us, as long as we work with our experience rather than rejecting what karma brings us. But in order not to reject what is arising, we need to apply patience. This is what makes patience such a crucial aspect of our spiritual path. It is the only wise and effective approach to working skillfully with our karma and transforming negativity into positivity. To let our ordinary habits dictate how we respond to our ripening karma is to go through life just like anyone who has never heard the dharma. For example, if someone treats you unjustly and you fall back on your right to respond with aggression, become obsessed with removing that threat from your life, or make a tremendous effort to get justice or even the score, you may achieve your temporary goal, but you will be sowing the same old karmic seeds again and again and entrenching yourself deeper in the karmic cycle. That is the natural course for someone who acts mainly from habit and confusion, and our conventional culture supports this approach. But if you have dharma in your life, you can do better.

To practice the dharma successfully requires persistent effort in working with the mind. We must understand that we have the choice to respond conventionally or unconventionally. The latter choice is to apply the wisdom of dharma to our state of mind and our situation, whatever they may be.

Many people have the notion that as soon as they start looking at dharma books, keeping a shrine, or identifying themselves in some way as Buddhists, then spiritual growth will happen automatically. Such an unrealistic assumption can make it seem like it's the fault of the dharma if they don't make progress. Unfortunately, this happens often.

To benefit from the dharma, we have to be there every step of the way, working with our own minds and emotions, starting from a basis of self-reflection and profound acceptance. As it is said, "Dharma must be practiced according to dharma. Otherwise dharma itself can be a cause of suffering and lower rebirth." Teachers and teachings can give us a map to inner peace or even complete enlightenment; shrines, rituals, and formal practices are a great support; but the process is a completely internal and individual one. We have to follow the road ourselves.

For this reason, creativity is an indispensable ingredient for the practitioner. Though the dharma is vast and profound—and must be practiced according to dharma itself—our practice is incomplete unless we make use of our own creativity, which brings the teachings to our personal experience. To lay the groundwork for the creative process of dharma, we must first take the time to see what is happening in our minds. This involves identifying our thoughts, emotions, and attitudes and understanding what their effects are likely to be. From there, we reflect on what needs to be adjusted and how we can make that adjustment through our knowledge of dharma. We should do this not only every day on the meditation cushion but also whenever we are confronted or challenged. This approach has to be our continual starting point.

Different situations require different approaches. You should feel the liberty to choose from among your many dharmic tools, to experiment creatively and learn from your mistakes. After all, no one knows your mind better than you do. No one can look into your mind at this very moment and experience it with you. No one else is experiencing your karma in exactly the same way you are. Others may be going through similar outer events and having similar thoughts and emotions, but their experience is not yours, and yours is not theirs. If our only tool is to imitate outwardly what others—even great sages—have done before, we will often find ourselves at a loss. Every situation we are in is new, every moment fresh. Most of the time there is no person or book that can tell us exactly what to do. If we think there is or should be, we will probably end up resorting to conventional means rather than the dharma.

For example, you may be feeling frustrated or judgmental toward someone close to you. From the teachings you've heard, it's not obvious what the antidote is. At that point, you might feel discouraged. Instead of figuring out a creative approach or simply experimenting, you might fall back on the thought, *In time, this will go away*. It's true that your pain will go away in time. And it can be helpful and reassuring to have such a thought. But if you just leave it there and let things play out—without your involvement, so to speak—you are not taking advantage of the dharma or using your creativity. Practicing dharma is by no means passive. In this example, the relief from frustration would be time's doing, not your doing as a practitioner.

A wise person like Shantideva would self-reflect more deeply and determine where the frustration was coming from. In this way, he would have a precise target to aim at. From there, he would look into his toolbox of skillful means and apply the most appropriate antidote, tailoring it to meet the specific occasion. If the first antidote didn't work, he would try a second. In this way, he would learn from his painful emotion and transform it into wisdom and compassion, which would benefit himself and others. This is an example of taking responsibility for your own mind and emotions with self-reflection as a basis. In this way, you can integrate dharma into your life step-by-step.

I recently heard of an incident that took place in eastern Tibet. A married couple who had children attempted to rob another family by breaking into their house. When they unexpectedly came across the parents of the other family, they killed them. For this crime, they were sentenced to death according to Chinese law. But the teenage daughter of the murdered couple pled for forgiveness of her parents' killers, thus sparing them from the death penalty. In making her case, she presented two pieces of reasoning: first, executing the murderers would not bring back her parents; and second, it would make their children orphans just like herself. When I heard this story, I thought the young girl must have been an incredible practitioner in her last life. She was able to get beyond the first round of intensely disturbing thoughts and painful emotions that must have arisen in her mind and being when her parents were killed. Then she was able to get past conventional ways of looking at the situation, such as "justice must be served." It took tremendous insight and skill for her to navigate beyond these two reactions and find a way to move forward with tsewa and wisdom. For me, this teenager's response to her parents' murder is an incredible example of working with pain creatively and courageously.

As Marpa the Translator said to his illustrious disciple Milarepa, "Son, do not view pain as negative." This is a very profound teaching. If we have a connection to the dharma, pain helps us deepen our practice and learn the wisdom of the dharma through our own experience. We come to discover that overcoming suffering is really about changing our mental attitude, changing the position of our mind. This insight builds our confidence and self-esteem. As we try this once, twice, we see it is possible, and a new pathway becomes established. It takes great confidence to become a bodhisattva. It takes high self-esteem to be able to love the people who cause you the most pain. Because they know how much negative karma these people are destined to reap, bodhisattvas make even more prayers for them than they do for the people who treat them with kindness. All of these benefits come from having a positive attitude toward suffering, from putting more emphasis on long-term growth than on short-term comfort.

This attitude may seem difficult, and it is. But it is neither unrealistic nor beyond our capacity. Say you need open-heart surgery to save your life. You need to let yourself be cut open, let your ribs be spread apart, let your heart be stopped, let a machine pump your blood, let the doctors carve and snip your heart with knives and scissors, let yourself be wired and stitched back together. You are willing and able to endure such harsh treatment and severe pain because it will enable you to go on living. Not only is it completely normal to go through this kind of ordeal, if you decide you'd rather avoid the pain of heart surgery and instead let your life be cut short, most people will think you've gone crazy and try to talk sense into you.

For many of us, mental suffering is harder to handle than most forms of physical pain. This is because the former brings up confusion, which makes us succumb easily to the power of our habitual emotional reactions and old ruts. But if we adopt the view that mental pain is not something to fear or reject, then our minds will become more flexible, and we will become more proficient at appreciating adverse circumstances and transforming them into a benefit for our path. Then our mental health regimen will be less like open-heart surgery and more like a dietary change, such as giving up excessively rich foods. If you love greasy hamburgers and your doctor tells you that your arteries are getting clogged, you will most likely sacrifice your daily hamburger gladly. Once you get used to your new diet and see how it improves your health, you will not even be tempted to go back.

In a similar way, if we adopt a more welcoming attitude to mental pain and adverse circumstances, we will come to see for ourselves how malleable the mind is. This ongoing direct experience will provide us with constant encouragement to go forward in our practice. We will then have firsthand knowledge to corroborate these famous words of the Buddha: "If you work with your mind, it becomes your greatest ally and will serve you well. If you don't work with your mind, it becomes your greatest enemy and will torment you tremendously."

EIGHT

Working with Jealousy

76
When others take delight
In giving praise to those endowed with talents,
Why, O mind, do you not find
A joy likewise in praising them?

With this verse, Shantideva begins to explore another form of yi midewe ze, the disturbance we feel when our adversaries, rivals, or those we simply do not like get what they want. In this section, he takes a look at the emotion of jealousy.

The language of Buddhism classifies the primary disturbing emotions as the "five poisons," or *kleshas*, a word that comes from Sanskrit. These are attachment, aggression, pride, jealousy, and *timuk*. This last word is often translated from Tibetan as "ignorance" or "stupidity," but the literal meaning is "deep mental fog." This fog is the root of our suffering and the starting point of the misunderstanding already referred to—that we have a singular, unchanging, autonomous self.

Timuk prevents us from seeing through the delusion that propels us to cling to this self. Then, because we habitually believe in and cling to this projection of an intrinsic self, we feel compelled to cherish and protect it at all times. In this way, timuk is the source of the other four poisons. Our foggy confusion around this sense of self is what leads to all our painful states of mind and emotions; from those come all our actions that harm us and others, keeping us bound within samsara. This is the basic formula that describes the deluded mind of beings in samsara.

Attachment comes from cherishing this sense of self: we become attached to objects—people, things, conditions—that we think will make the self happy, and we work hard to pull these things closer. We become aggressive to protect this sense of self when we sense it is threatened or when anything hinders our attachments being met. We work hard to push these people, things, and conditions away. The pain of attachment and aggression is basically the pain of not getting what we want and the pain of getting what we don't want. Pride or arrogance is an extension of attachment because it is a more developed form of self-cherishing. Similarly, jealousy is an extension of aggression. We are protecting ourselves against the feeling that others are doing as well as or better than we are. We wish that were not the case.

See if you can identify this almost visceral pull and push with things. Notice when you try to pull in things that you think support your sense of self and push away things that threaten you. Start with small things to see if you can identify these tendencies. Then further challenge yourself to notice what's happening when you are upset about something. Take a pause in the storylines and reflect. Ask yourself if you are trying to cherish or protect your sense of self. Is that urge mixed in with all your thoughts and feelings?

If you can simply notice and identify which tendency has been activated, without any judgment of yourself, you may find a great sense of relief. Just seeing it—and being able to take a breath and let go of it—will soothe your mind. You will likely find yourself with a clearer head, able to sort out how best to remedy the situation at hand. Any time you are engaged in neurotic self-protection, you have a chance to apply patience, which can open up a treasure trove of wisdom inside you.

In this light, Shantideva now begins to discuss patience as an antidote to jealousy. Why do people praise each other? Generally praise is an expression of inspiration, connection, and joy. We see an action or a quality that we appreciate, and we show our appreciation to the person who performs that action or possesses that quality through some form of praise. It gives us a feeling of pleasure to acknowledge another person who touches us in this way. So Shantideva is asking here, when you see that happening with others, why not join in with their pleasure? Why not enjoy the positive emotion of the one who is praising? If you have trouble joining in fully because you don't believe in the praise, that's all right. But in that case, you can at least not get irritated.

If you do get irritated, you should know that under the surface there is something extra happening inside you. There is no good reason to be offended because the praise is not directed at you. The person giving praise is not trying to insult or provoke you. It may feel that way, but some self-reflection will show you this is not the case. If you penetrate your deep mental fog, you will most likely discover that your ego is feeling a bit threatened because you are feeling ignored.

When we are jealous, we don't have the heart to bear any glory or appreciation unless it is related to us. If the world showers acknowledgment on someone else, instead of joining in with the world, we make it a personal issue. We think the recipient of praise doesn't deserve it. Why? If you look, you will be hard-pressed to find a rational reason. It is usually because your ego feels left out. So you turn the acknowledgment of another into a personal offence. This can happen on a very subtle level.

When you catch yourself having this attitude, it is a great opportunity to turn inward and look at the state of your heart. If you look openly, you will discover that your heart has become quite small. Unless you remedy this painful state of affairs, you will start to lose your self-respect and the respect of others, especially if you speak or act from this place of pettiness.

Self-recognition doesn't have to come with critical self-judgment. You can have some humor about the fascinating workings of your mind. How ironic that you want others to be happy for you, but you're so unwilling to be happy for anyone else. It is very freeing to be able to admit this is where you are caught at the moment. Then you can have a good chuckle and naturally come to agree that it's really in your best interest to open your heart and join in with acknowledging others. Or if that's not possible at the moment, why not at least let the praisers and the praised have their enjoyment without taking it so personally?

77
The pleasure that is gained therefrom
Itself gives rise to blameless happiness.
It's urged on us by all the holy ones,
And is the perfect way of winning others.

If we seek happiness through external, conventional means, our efforts generally involve difficult labor on many levels and bondage to our attachments. We have to drive ourselves forward with great determination to overcome all the obstacles that keep coming up. For example, if we seek happiness by making a lot of money or coming to a position of power and influence, that will most likely involve taking part in some sort of negative behavior, such as cunning and deceit. Then, in the end, it's not at all certain we will attain our object of desire or achieve our goal. Even if we do, we quickly find another desire and then another. It's like drinking salty water—the more we get, the more we want.

Then there is another problem. Before we got what we wanted, we could at least enjoy our passion—our daydreaming about how we would get it and how wonderful it would be to have it. But once we do have it, we often find it's not what we hoped it would be. The object of our desire may well become an object of disappointment, anxiety, or even disgust. This is one of the many sad, repetitive stories of samsara.

This is why the Buddha said that sympathetic joy—the vicarious happiness of rejoicing for others—is the supreme joy. It is the cleanest form of joy because it is unrelated to the eight worldly concerns, which all have the sense of self at the center. It is free from attachment, aversion, and all other states of mind and emotions that disturb us. Sympathetic joy also takes little effort. At this very moment, we can think of any number of people who are experiencing good fortune, fulfillment, or pleasure, whether in their worldly lives, on the spiritual path, or both. The only effort we need to make is in remembering that they are exactly like us in desiring happiness and enjoying whatever good circumstances arise in their lives.

In the case of praise, there are four ways we can find sympathetic joy. Focusing on the praiser, we can rejoice in their ability to recognize qualities to appreciate. We can also rejoice in their pleasure in praising. Focusing on the recipient, we can rejoice in their qualities and in their pleasure in receiving praise and recognition. So even if we're not directly involved, we can derive a great deal of happiness from just one act of praise by thinking this way. The only obstacle is the ego and its tendency to cry out for attention when it thinks it is being ignored. But when we're aware of this tendency and see through the ego's demands, it loses its power to rule us and undermine our better qualities. Self-centered mind can only cause us harm when it is left unexamined and allowed to dictate according to its whims.

Shantideva's other point in this verse is that rejoicing is the best way of winning people over. People try so hard to make an impression on the world and on others. For example, you may build a magnificent house that has more space and more amazing features than anyone could ever need. Since you are mainly doing it to impress others, you will feel disappointed if nobody praises your house or gives you their approval. If you bring friends over and they are critical or indifferent, you will feel disappointed, hurt, and rejected. You may expect them to be delighted by your spectacular kitchen with its marble slab central island and massive enamel stove, but all they do is point out that the lighting is too harsh. This is probably the result of jealousy or competitiveness inside them. But if someone comes along who is very impressed— and not just impressed, but genuinely happy for you—then you feel and appreciate their support. You feel a sense of fulfillment and solidarity with that person. You will naturally feel drawn to them. Think about this example seriously.

Sympathetic joy doesn't come to us automatically. Because of our attachment to the self, jealousy usually comes more naturally. But we can cultivate our ability to rejoice through practice. This begins with reflecting on the pitfalls of jealousy, which is such a pointless, ineffectual suffering. Jealousy is self-inflicted torture without any positive aspect. It doesn't even bring any of the acknowledgment the ego craves. On the contrary, it makes us feel inside that we are even less worthy of praise or appreciation. Nor does it bridge the gap between us and those of whom we are jealous—people who have good fortune because of their past good deeds. In fact, it only depletes our merit, perpetuates our feeling that we are lacking something, and makes us increasingly miserable the more we indulge in it.

If we reflect on the hazards of jealousy, we will be motivated to be vigilant about its occurrence in our mind. When jealousy does arise, we will feel inspired to reflect on how we are getting caught in the ego's self-centered demands. Then we will be able to see the irony and generate the positive emotion of sympathetic joy, rejoicing in the fortune and goodness of others.

In this way, we can change many of our relationships for the better. For example, if someone doesn't like you, and instead of resenting them, you contemplate and rejoice in their good qualities objectively, this change in your own attitude may well soften their mind. Then they may come around to you as a friend. If you were the black sheep of your family, and then you cultivate genuine sympathetic joy for your family members, you may become the white sheep. Or if you were the oddball among your circle of friends, in time you may become the most sought-out member of your group. Sympathetic joy will make you more trusted and sought out in any community. Its natural effect is to make people feel close to you. This is especially important for bodhisattvas, who magnetize people not in order to feel more popular, but so they may benefit others with the dharma.

78

"But they're the ones who'll have the happiness," you say.
If this then is a joy you would resent,
Abandon paying wages and returning favors.
You will be the loser—both in this life and the next!

Resenting others' happiness is an unhealthy mind-set that brings us much suffering, both in the present and as a result of the negative karma it creates. It eats away at our decency and ruins our relationships. Objectively speaking, this attitude is as unreasonable as refusing to pay, or even appreciate, someone who works hard for you because it bothers you too much to see someone else happy. Anyone can realize that such an attitude is absurd. Of course, we almost always feel joy when we reward someone who has worked hard for us. Their joy becomes our joy. In the same way, the happiness of someone being praised can also become our own happiness. In the case of vicarious happiness, we don't even have to spend any money.

This reasoning may strike us as simple-minded or ordinary, but we should honestly reflect on how much we suffer from jealousy and competitiveness. Then we should consider what it would be like to be free of that nagging, petty mind. Contemplating Shantideva's wisdom and applying it creatively to our lives will make such freedom a genuine possibility.

79

When praise is heaped upon your qualities,
You're keen that others should be pleased thereby.
But when the compliment is paid to others,
You feel no inclination to rejoice as well.

When someone praises you—even if it's your sworn enemy—you feel good. You are always happy to be praised and perhaps even more so if the praise comes from your enemy. You think, *Wow, I must be really good! This is not my mother praising me, it's my sworn enemy!* The irony here is that your enemy is also experiencing joy—probably even greater joy than you are—because appreciating others' qualities is a joyful experience. In this case, you are happy about your enemy's joy.

This logic exposes how twisted our minds can be. We are happy when our adversaries recognize our qualities but deny that very joy to ourselves. This is as nonsensical as watching with approval as your adversary enjoys a plate of delicious food but then rejecting that same food when it's offered to you. Why would you deprive yourself of the chance to enjoy good food?

When you are happy on someone else's behalf, that happiness belongs to you. The only reason we would deny ourselves that happiness is our enslavement to our self-importance. But when we see through our ego's faulty perspective, we can learn to derive joy from anyone's qualities, achievements, or successes, even those of people who have hurt us.

When we become proficient in the practice of sympathetic joy, facing and overcoming our jealousy becomes an immense delight. The contrast and transition between the two emotions makes the bliss of the sympathetic joy even more vivid. It is similar to recovering from the flu. When we feel well, we don't usually notice the naturally abiding bliss of a healthy body. But when we've had the flu for a week and then start to feel better, the natural bliss in our body comes out vividly. Even before we've fully recovered, we enjoy the deep delight of the contrast between sickness and health.

80
You who want the happiness of beings
Have wished to be enlightened for their sake.
So why should others irk you when
They find some pleasure for themselves?

81
And if you claim to wish that beings
Be enlightened, honored by the triple world,

When petty marks of favor come their way,
Why are you so discomforted?

82
When dependents who rely on you,
To whom you are obliged to give support,
Find for themselves the means of livelihood,
Will you not be happy, will you once again be angry?

83
If even this you do not want for beings,
How could you want Buddhahood for them?
And how can anyone have bodhicitta
Who is angry when another prospers?

The mission of the bodhisattva is to lead every sentient being—
without exception—out of the suffering of samsara and into the limitless peace and joy of enlightenment. For this purpose, bodhisattvas generate bodhicitta, the wish to attain their own enlightenment on behalf
of others. This is our ultimate aim in studying texts such as Shantideva's.

If we consider ourselves to be following the same path the bodhisattvas have tread, we should continually examine our thoughts and
emotions to see if they are congruent with the vast motivation of
bodhicitta. To be able to rejoice only on behalf of certain beings but
feel jealous in regard to others goes against the fundamental principle of equality—that all beings are equal in their longing to be happy
and free from suffering. It also goes against the practice of impartial
loving-kindness, in which we wish for all beings to have happiness
and its causes.

The sign of proficiency in loving-kindness is regarding the happiness of others as our own happiness. When we are jealous and envious, we are against the happiness of others. If we are against their
experience of relative happiness, then how can we be in favor of their
attaining enlightenment, the ultimate happiness? These two mind-sets

are diametrically opposed to one another. Bodhicitta and jealousy are incompatible.

When beings attain enlightenment, they become just like the Buddha, who was honored by the entire world. How can we wish them to enter such an exalted state when we don't even want them to be appreciated by others or hear a single word of praise? Isn't that a ridiculous contradiction? Since it is rare to find any joy in samsara, how can we not be glad when the beings we've committed to help experience a few glimpses of happiness here and there? This position is similar to raising your children, devoting tremendous attention and energy to their well-being, and then becoming upset when they go off on their own and do well for themselves. What kind of parent is disturbed by an outcome like that?

As developing bodhisattvas, we all forget ourselves and indulge in this kind of hypocritical behavior from time to time. We are all in the process of changing our egocentric habits and replacing them with wisdom and tsewa. These stanzas, just like all the verses in *The Way of the Bodhisattva*, encourage us to look carefully and openly at what we are thinking and doing on an ongoing basis. We need to uncover our hidden faults and identify their root—our self-centered stance and the ego's habitual mechanism of trying to protect and cherish itself at all costs.

To transform our habitual egotistical tendencies into wisdom, we need to take the teachings and use them in a productive internal dialogue run by our wisdom mind. Looking at the arising of jealousy as a great opportunity to learn and grow will make this process a joy. By contemplating the logic Shantideva presents, we can put things in perspective and come to think and act in a way that enhances, rather than sabotages, our bodhicitta.

84

If someone else receives a gift,
Or if that gift stays in the benefactor's house,
In neither case will it be yours—
So, given or withheld, why is it your concern?

Say you and your good friend are hanging out together. A mutual friend visiting from out of town stops by. The mutual friend brings a gift for your friend but nothing for you. Say the gift is a nice pair of dangling earrings. Right away you feel bummed out. You think, *Why didn't she bring me anything? She's my friend too. She even knows I like dangling earrings!*

You almost feel like you have lost something precious, but Shantideva points out how irrational this thinking is. The earrings were never yours to begin with. Why does it matter to you if your friend received them or they stayed in the mutual friend's drawer? If the gift had been promised to you, that would be one thing, but those dangling earrings were never destined to come into your possession. So why not be happy for your friend and rejoice in seeing her wear her new jewelry? Why not see the humor in how your ego, like a spoiled child, is always crying to be at the center of everything? Why not free yourself from such a limited point of view and instead find a source of sympathetic joy?

85

All your merit and the faith of others,
All your sterling qualities—why throw them all away?
Not holding on to what might bring you riches,
Tell me, why are you not angry at yourself?

86

Not only do you feel no sorrow
For the evils you have done,
You even wish to match yourself
With those whose merit has been earned!

If you get jealous and envious of someone else receiving praise, acknowledgment, a gift, a promotion, or anything else you desire, not only will that not get you what you want, but your reaction may also ruin your chances of getting such things in the future. Instead, think about it this way. Nothing happens at random. The person you are jealous of must in some way deserve what they've received, meaning they must have some good qualities or some merit from the past.

In other religious teachings, it is believed that a god or creator is the force that operates the universe. According to the Buddhadharma, the universe is run by karma, the law of cause and effect. A well-known teaching uses the analogy of a tree: "If the root is medicinal, the trunk and leaves will be medicinal. If the root is poisonous, the trunk and leaves will be poisonous." The teachings also say that the one who sows the seed is the one who reaps the fruit. This means that your altruistic or harmful deed will have its primary result in your own future. If you act based on altruism, you will be the one to experience the positive effect of your action. Conversely, any positive experience you have now must be the result of an altruistic action from your own past—if not in this lifetime then in a past life.

If you're not experiencing the same level of good fortune as someone else, it must mean that you're lacking the other person's good qualities or merit, which have brought about certain causes and conditions in their lives. But this is not something to despair about. It is not a permanent situation. Instead of getting jealous, why not cultivate those qualities yourself? Why not gather merit and create the proper conditions through your understanding of cause and effect? Genuinely rejoicing or being generous and good-hearted in any way—especially when these feelings are based on the altruistic vision of bodhicitta—gathers tremendous merit. Now you have a chance to rejoice, so you should take it. If you don't grab this perfect opportunity that has fallen into your lap, you are throwing away a chance to sow positive seeds for the future, not to mention the soothing effect it can have on your present mind.

NINE

Not Taking Pleasure
in Others' Pain

87
If unhappiness befalls your enemies,
Why should this be cause for your rejoicing?
The wishes of your mind alone,
Will not in fact contrive their injury.

Now we move into another group of the seventy-two ways
we get disturbed. The next three verses are about our reactions to unpleasant things happening to our "enemies." This category
includes people we feel competitive with or simply don't like. In this
stanza, Shantideva asks what it is that makes us happy when we hear
about their pain. Does their misfortune benefit us in some way? Are
we enjoying some perverse satisfaction that our malevolent aspirations have come true? Is it that we wished for them to suffer and that
wish has been fulfilled?

Here is an important point to understand: this thinking is illogical. Beings experience suffering due to their own past actions, their
karma. What happens to other people has nothing to do with our
own negative wishes for them. It may be that we have no conscious
wishes for harm to come to them, but when they do suffer pain or
misfortune, we feel a subtle sense of satisfaction because of our past
resentment or pain. It feels like a relief, as if we're finally scratching

an itch that has been bothering us for some time. If that is our feeling, we should ask ourselves whether this is a noble state of mind. Does it have any kindness and compassion in it? Isn't this the opposite of bodhicitta? On top of that, we should reflect on how holding on to such states will only disturb our own minds and cause all sorts of suffering to fall upon our heads.

88

And if your hostile wishes were to bring them harm,
Again, what cause of joy is that to you?
"Why, then I would be satisfied!"—are these your thoughts?
Is anything more ruinous than that?

89

Caught upon the hook, unbearable and sharp,
Cast by the fisherman, my own defilements,
I'll be flung into the cauldrons of the pit,
And surely boiled by all the janitors of hell!

If our wishes somehow did lead to our enemy or rival's suffering, how could we truly rejoice in that? The outcome might make us happy in the heat of aggression or jealousy, but if joy remains when our mind has calmed down, what does that say about our heart? For an aspiring bodhisattva, the emotion of schadenfreude—pleasure that comes from someone else's pain—is a pleasure we should forsake immediately.

There is the famous Tibetan story of the two scholarly monks. One monk heard a juicy piece of gossip about the other monk. He said to his attendant, "Make some nice tea. I have good news to share." When they sat down to their tea, the attendant asked what the good news was. The monk said, "I heard our rival has a mistress!" When another teacher, who had more wisdom than either of the monks, heard this story, he asked, "Which of the two monks committed the worse deed?" One monk may have given in to his desire and broken his vow of celibacy, but the other one reveled in the downfall and weakness of another.

Malevolent wishes for others—whether or not we are conscious of them—inevitably lead to our own misfortune and deep unhappiness. This is clear from countless stories from history, novels, and movies. Cunning people with evil intent may seem to be doing well at the beginning of the story, but in the end, they fail to accomplish what they desire most and everything they dread comes back to them.

Our schadenfreude is like a fisherman and our harmful wishes are like a baited hook. For the small satisfaction we derive from tasting the bait, so much negativity is unleashed from within. This will lead to many painful consequences in this and future lifetimes. Even more tragically, our ill intent will grind our peaceful heart and tsewa into dust.

Here you have an opportunity to self-reflect. If you find such hidden faults within, acknowledge and regret them. Let go of these unconscious mind-sets through the contemplations already laid out. Try to do this without the unnecessary and detrimental addition of self-loathing. You can avoid that painful hindrance by understanding that these tendencies are not your true self.

Our true self wants to awaken to attain enlightenment for the benefit of all beings. It is for this very reason that we feel uncomfortable when we see this tendency toward schadenfreude in ourselves. It is also why we immediately feel regret. Even the embarrassment that may arise within is a sign that our true self aspires to something greater.

For this aspiration to blossom and grow, becoming aware of your hidden faults is a great blessing. But make sure not to identify with those faults. Instead, take this opportunity to identify with your wisdom mind rather than follow the rut of ignorance. Engender a sense of joy in this process of wearing away your self-importance to reveal your true heart of bodhicitta.

TEN

Practicing Patience When We Don't Get What We Want

90
Veneration, praise, and fame
Serve not to increase merit or my span of life,
Bestowing neither health nor strength
And nothing for the body's ease.

Here Shantideva begins to talk about cultivating patience toward those who prevent us from getting what we desire. This is another category of yi midewe ze from the seventy-two ways we get disturbed.

We all want some measure of praise, fame, or at least acknowledgment for ourselves and our loved ones. However, if we are too passionate about these things, we will inevitably be angry at anyone who hinders our achieving them. We should ask ourselves whether these worldly concerns are worth getting upset about. Why do we have these desires in the first place? Have we thought this through with our rational mind, or are we simply following conventional values and being influenced by cultural peer pressure? Have we even taken the time to ask ourselves if these things truly have value for us? Furthermore, what do praise, fame, and acknowledgment really do for us?

We generate merit when our hearts are imbued with tsewa and our minds are concerned with the well-being of others. Seeking renown, pleasant words in our ears, and VIP service comes from a narrow mind-set based on cherishing the small, singular self. If we already enjoy the approval of the world, that is the fruit of our past merit. But by clinging to our status with so much attachment, we actually waste that merit and sow no positive seeds for the future.

Our quest for praise and fame also does nothing positive for our health. For example, some people work incredibly hard for these things, often upward of sixty to seventy hours a week. As they begin to achieve their aims, they have to work even harder. They go on and on, almost blinded by their drive and attachments. They may keep going even after having one or two heart attacks, working day and night with a pacemaker keeping them alive. Even if you become the CEO of a major company, is that kind of stress worth it? What's the use of becoming so successful or famous if there's a good chance you'll become incapacitated or even drop dead?

Achieving these worldly concerns brings no benefit for our mental strength either. On the contrary, our growing attachment, based on our investment in achieving something for the singular self, only makes us weaker. We see this all the time. As they become successful, people who used to be friendly and carefree become anxious, reactive, aggressive, and even paranoid. They lose control of their minds, and their emotions tend to run wild.

If we want to be intelligent people who know how to take care of our own well-being, we need to examine our desires and drives clearly and objectively. Then we can ask ourselves whether we want to spend what remains of our lives—a span of time that is completely uncertain—in such pursuits. If we conclude that our time would be better spent cultivating bodhicitta and doing the practices that will lead to enlightenment, then praise and fame will not lure us so strongly. Since they do nothing for our personal spiritual path, we may even come to see them as a distraction and a nuisance.

Even if we do attain some measure of renown or fame, we won't be able to take it with us when we die. Not only that, but after fifty or a hundred years, will we even be remembered for what we worked so hard to be acknowledged for? Probably not. If we want to leave a legacy, we have a much better chance by working on our bodhicitta and developing peaceful hearts that can bring genuine benefit to beings.

91

If I am wise in what is good for me,
I'll ask what benefit these bring.
For if it's entertainment I desire,
I might as well resort to alcohol and cards!

What do you really want from your life? If your aim is to be a wise person with a compassionate and peaceful heart, then how does it benefit you to try and attract praise and fame? Do these worldly concerns help you learn how to self-reflect, to discern what actions are helpful from what actions are harmful? Do they help you become the independent, awakened person you want to be, someone who is not easily seduced by the whims of conventional beliefs regarding the causes of happiness?

The cultural consensus is that the more praise and fame we have, the happier we will be. But imagine what it's like to be a big movie star or a cultural icon whose face everyone recognizes. These people cannot be free members of society. They are followed around by paparazzi on the lookout for any teardrop, any sign of weakness, any hint that their relationship may be going sour. There's a saying in India: whether a cage is made of iron or gold, it's still a cage. The kind of metal makes no difference to the bird.

We want praise, fame, and acknowledgment because of the temporary pleasure they give to the ego. The passion to cherish the self in these ways is a form of addiction. We need it to be satisfied over and over. We seek out the fix of others' approval or praise, but once we get it, we are only fulfilled for a short while before falling prey to our insecurities. The fix wears off, and we are on to the next one.

If our aim is just to fulfill an addiction to temporary pleasure, then we might as well go for things like alcohol and gambling. This is a stark comparison for Shantideva to make, especially since he was originally speaking to monks. His point is to make it absolutely clear how self-destructive it is to base our lives on feeding our ultimately futile desires.

92
I lose my life, my wealth I squander,
All for reputation's sake.
What use are words, and whom will they delight
When I am dead and in my grave?

Those who are enchanted by renown and reputation will go to almost any length to achieve these aims. Some people risk their lives in war because of the cultural consensus that places value on giving one's life on the battlefield. Some put all their time and effort into promoting themselves, especially nowadays when everybody can publicize their own image through Instagram, TikTok, Facebook, and YouTube. Some lie, cheat, steal, and even kill to impress others and prevent negative information about them from leaking out.

When I think of the futility of fame, Ronald Reagan often comes to mind as a good example. He enjoyed great renown most of his life and for eight years was the most recognizable and powerful person in the world. Then he got Alzheimer's disease and didn't even know who he was. What could all that admiration and fame do for him then?

Say you are a bird among a flock that has landed on a field and leisurely commence eating some grain. If the bird in front of you drops dead, you will be concerned about what it just ate. You will most likely fly off to a different section of the field, to where the other birds are having better reactions to their food. Here, as so often in his book, Shantideva is encouraging us to be like a cautious bird, to observe cause and effect and make intelligent choices from there.

93
Children can't help crying when
Their sandcastles come crumbling down.

My mind is so like them
When praise and reputation start to fail.

Children build sandcastles, not realizing that they will soon be destroyed. When the fatal wave comes, they are so dismayed that they burst into tears. When it comes to praise and reputation, we are just like these children. Many adults fall into deep depressions and even commit suicide when their reputations are ruined and they start hearing nasty words instead of glowing praise.

To the enlightened beings who see through the eight worldly concerns and the seventy-two ways we get disturbed, we struggling adults are as silly and ignorant as children at the beach. We will remain this way until we also see through our constant struggle. This will involve first seeing those concerns for what they really are, and then using our insight as a moment of awakening to set ourselves firmly on the bodhisattva path.

94
Short-lived sound, devoid of intellect,
Can never in itself intend to praise me.
I say that it's the joy that others take in me,
It's this that is the cause of my delight.

95
But what is it to me if others take delight
In someone else, or even in myself?
Their pleasure's theirs and theirs alone.
No part of it is felt by me.

96
If I am happy at the joy of those who take delight,
Then everyone should be a source of joy to me.
When people take delight in others
Why am I not happy at their pleasure?

Now Shantideva tries to get to the bottom of what makes us covet praise in the first place. Why does praise give us so much pleasure? Is it the sound of the words? If that were the case, it would be so simple. We could record ourselves singing our own praises and play the recording as often as we wanted!

The fact that this wouldn't be satisfying proves that we are after something more than mere sound. What is that? You could say it's not the words, it's the mind behind those words. You want the person to like you, to admire you, to feel good about you. But Shantideva points out that these good feelings are actually the other person's experience and theirs alone. You only experience your own mind, not the minds of other beings.

You might reply, "That's true, but I am doing the practice of rejoicing. Their good feelings about me bring them happiness. From that I can derive a sense of sympathetic joy." But if you have the ability to make others' happiness into your own, then you can be happy whatever the object of their joy, whether they like you or something else entirely. So why be fixated on hearing nice words about yourself? There are always plenty of people being praised and honored. Why not take delight in that? The reasoning here is just like that in the previous verses (76 through 86) about not being disturbed when good things happen to your enemies or rivals.

Shantideva is a master at unmasking our self-deception and showing us how we defend the ego with illogical logic. If we are only happy when we ourselves are praised, that can't be true sympathetic joy. We haven't yet developed proficiency in this skill. Someone who is not a carpenter can't build a house by pretending to be a carpenter. Similarly, someone who hasn't cultivated the skill of rejoicing can't feel inner peace by pretending to rejoice. We have to walk the walk, not just talk the talk.

97
The satisfaction that is mine
From thinking, "I am being praised,"

Is unacceptable to common sense
And nothing but the antics of a silly child.

98
Praise and compliments distract me,
Sapping my revulsion with samsara.
I start to envy others their good qualities
And thus all excellence is ruined.

Craving praise is nonsensical and silly because it doesn't bring us any real joy. One day, someone praises you, and you feel delighted. Naturally, you hope for more praise. But the next day the same person doesn't praise you, and you feel disappointed or insecure, or you wonder if you did something wrong. One day, someone approves of you, and you feel happy. The next day they don't voice their approval, and you feel upset or shaky. One day, you consider the person to be your friend. The next day, you consider them to be almost a threat. When you get hooked into these hopes and disappointments, your mind and emotions become like a rollercoaster. Don't think this has to be a conscious occurrence. It could all be happening at a subtle level.

Some people, through the merit of their past deeds, experience long periods of approval and renown. But even that status is not so desirable when we examine it. When everything goes our way, it becomes almost impossible to remember that we're still caught in the overall mechanism of samsara. We are still attached to a self that does not exist in the way we think it does. From this basic misunderstanding, all the disturbing states of mind—attachment, aggression, and the rest—will inevitably arise. These will naturally lead us to act in self-centered ways, and these actions will create the negative karma for many painful experiences to arise inevitably in the future.

But we are easily fooled. Good circumstances, especially if they last for years or decades, prevent us from seeing this underlying process of creating suffering for ourselves and others. At some point, however, the suffering of samsara will make itself visible, and we will be unprepared for our precipitous fall.

We see this happen all the time. People who have enjoyed fame and good standing for many years suddenly find some past wrong-doing exposed and lose their popularity and reputation overnight. Those who have had a lifetime of good fortune often have the greatest difficulty facing the decline of their bodies and abilities, not to mention impending death. In their most helpless hour, they find themselves without the merit and strength to adapt. Then they may find themselves regretting their lives of distraction and self-indulgence. For this reason, dharma teachings always caution us about investing in samsaric happiness.

Receiving too much praise and approval also creates the pitfall of stirring up our competitiveness. We get attached to what we're good at—whatever it is that we have to show for ourselves. This can easily turn into a fixation that never leaves us. We become caught in this—and only this—pursuit. It becomes the entire justification for our existence. For example, making it to the top of our high school sport gives us a big rush, so we go for the college level. If we do well there, we go for the next level and the next. There is always another level to compete in. Instead of simply doing our best, we become preoccupied with how others are doing and how we can beat them in some way. In this way, our peers become our rivals. It comes to the point where we would rather see them fail than succeed.

If our area of interest is money, we single-mindedly push through all obstacles until we are rich. But our drive doesn't stop there. If we are in the circle of millionaires, we want to be in the circle of billionaires. And billionaires dream of more and more exclusive circles to compete in. Before we succumbed to these competitive drives, our heart was not in such a state of turmoil. But now, we can't escape these circles, which keep getting smaller and more confining.

This is how things naturally progress when we follow samsara's way—when we are ruled by convention and the values of the consensus. If we understand that this is what happens, we will think twice before indulging in competitive mind. Getting caught up in our endless drives saps our noble qualities, especially our ability to feel sympathetic joy. It isolates us from others and blocks the flow of our tsewa. It covers up who we truly are, burying our good nature under layers of confusion. The more we contemplate this topic, the less we will be enslaved by our desire for praise and fame. This is why Shantideva exhorts us to consider things honestly and with deep self-reflection.

99

Those who stay close by me, then,
To damage my good name and cut me down to size—
Are surely there protecting me
From falling into realms of grief.

100

For I am one who strives for freedom.
I must not be caught by wealth and honors.
How could I be angry with the ones
Who work to free me from my fetters?

101

They, like Buddha's very blessing,
Bar my way, determined as I am
To plunge myself headlong in sorrow:
How can I be angry with them?

One of the qualities that we spiritual practitioners could use more of is perseverance. The main reason we lack perseverance on the path is that we are so attached to our ordinary and often culturally instilled values—our lifestyle, our comforts, our relationships, our drives to cherish and protect this illusory self. But as we try to maintain our preferred world, years go by. Because the path is not our top priority, we fail to exert ourselves. Before we know it, this life will be over. If we don't pay attention, we will find ourselves on our deathbed, not having accomplished anything meaningful.

In these verses, Shantideva explains how adverse circumstances can rouse us from our complacency and save us from spinning endlessly and mindlessly in samsara. This is another example of the unconventional thinking so often employed in Buddhist mind training. As we have seen, worldly success and comfort can make us oblivious to the general suffering of samsara. Understanding this, we can regard anyone or anything that thwarts our conventional aims as an emissary of the loving buddhas and bodhisattvas. By disrupting our attachments to things that have no ultimate value, what seem to be obstacles to our happiness actually keep us from accumulating negative karma and turning this precious human life into a source of future misery. Therefore, instead of being angry with those who cut us down to size, we should appreciate them.

The analogy that comes to mind is having a wonderful dream about walking in a garden with a beautiful man or woman. You think you have reached the pinnacle of existence, but in reality, you are sleepwalking at the edge of a cliff. If someone wakes you up, you may at first be disappointed and angry, but as soon as you realize the danger you were in, your anger will turn to gratitude.

This is the attitude that practitioners such as Milarepa have cultivated. When his aunt and uncle stole his inheritance and turned his mother and sister into their servants, Milarepa first responded with hatred and sought revenge. Later, however, when he became a great yogin and his heart opened toward all sentient beings, he came to appreciate his aunt and uncle. He asked himself, *If it hadn't been for them, where would I be?*

This attitude—and the entire Patience Chapter itself—ultimately come down to working with the root of our suffering and painful states of mind, our attachment to our sense of a self and the ensuing obsession with cherishing and protecting this self. As we have seen, it is this self-importance that underlies all the seventy-two ways we get disturbed. Instead of enjoying the peace and radiance of a heart imbued with tsewa, we narrow our attention to what *I* want and what *I* don't want. We cling to all that we consider in our favor and try to annihilate all that is a threat to what we want. These are the ingredients that turn all the delicious food the phenomenal world offers us—the miracles of nature, art, our body, our senses, our wise and brilliant mind, and so on—into yi midewe ze, food that gives us mental and emotional indigestion.

Our self-importance is what makes us overreact and do all the things we regret. It's what makes a couple fight on their honeymoon and what makes a dinner guest ruin the party by shouting obscenities and throwing a champagne glass. Since this self-importance is clearly not our friend, we should not give it too much of our affection. When it wants to react, our best move is to say no, as a firm parent would say to a spoiled child.

The main reason we think and behave in destructive ways is that we're in some sort of pain. That pain is always rooted in our attachment to the self. But instead of reflecting on this to understand more deeply how this is so and what is going on, we skip to reacting. Thus, we feed our self-importance, encouraging it to grow stronger. The most efficient and direct way of working with the root of the problem is to deprive our self-importance of satisfaction. How do we do this? When it is in pain, instead of indulging it by reacting and running with our storylines and blame, we can let our self-importance have that pain.

Taking such an uncompromising approach may seem like a way of mistreating yourself or even an expression of self-aggression. But that is a misunderstanding of this instruction. In going against your self-importance, you are being tremendously kind to your deeper self, your true self, your tender heart of tsewa that longs to let its warmth flow exuberantly toward all sentient beings. Your self-importance usually commands your attention 100 percent and makes you believe that its needs are your deeper self's needs. But there is a distinction to identify and make here. If you stop identifying with the ignorant part of your mind—which is totally allied with the deluded clinging to a self that is not even there—and if you instead find some distance from your self-centered emotions and states of mind, you can become free of the tyranny of your self-importance.

By the way, when I say "you," please don't take it personally. I am talking to the universal you, which includes me as well. I am not addressing your true self and insulting your individual dignity. But I do mean to attack your ego, which is also my ego. In other words, I am insulting the universal ego—the mistaken habitual belief in a self and all that entails. Without insulting the universal ego, we can't get to the main point of the dharma, which is to reduce the self-importance that blocks our tsewa and produces all our suffering. So I occasionally find it useful to use the word "you." One can always make the teachings less personal, but this can be a way of sugarcoating them and diluting their effect. The word "we" may come across as friendlier, which is why I use it often in writing, but "you" tends to have more potency. This simple word can help you become aware of your hidden sore spots and your tendency to defend the ego.

If you would like to be free from these neuroses, it is necessary to first expose them and see them plainly and honestly for what they are. But as always, you should avoid the counterproductive sidetrack of self-loathing, which is based on the erroneous assumption that there is a self to loath. In fact, self-loathing could be considered a form of extra-strength ego. It is much simpler to see one's self-importance and acknowledge that you and all beings in samsara have this delusion of believing in a self. From there, you can aspire to find ways to let go of that clinging and, in its place, let your naturally present tsewa shine and grow.

Coming back to the point, what does it actually mean to let your self-importance have its pain? How do you do it? The practice is very simple. Just sit with your pain for however long you can. Sit with it and don't react one way or the other. I like to call this practice "simmering." Let your mind and heart simmer in that feeling for a little while without protecting or defending it with your thoughts and emotions. Try not to rescue your self-importance from its discomfort by resorting to aggression or distraction. Know that this process has something profound to teach you if you allow yourself to simmer in the experience.

Don't make a big deal about it, though. Regard the pain as nothing more serious than a bit of a headache. If you don't make a big deal about a bit of a headache, then you don't have to make a big deal about a bit of a heartache. We're not talking about the pain of a truly great loss or tragedy. This is just the day-to-day pain of your self-importance not being met in the way it expects or wants to be. These small occasions can teach you a great deal about yourself and be a source of tremendous growth. You have the ability to sit with it and not make it into a big deal.

Not only can you sit and simmer with it, you can do so joyfully because you know it is working against your self-importance in a very direct way. When you understand the great benefits of tolerating your pain—meaning letting yourself simmer—the pain itself becomes a form of bliss. This is similar to when athletes go through intense workouts that cause their muscles to burn. The athlete feels physical pain but experiences the sensations as ecstasy. As a practitioner, you can experience your own version of painful ecstasy by letting your self-importance simmer in its pain. It is really a marvelous experience.

For both athletes and courageous dharma practitioners, there is the recognition that one must go through pain in order to train toward a higher goal. In fact, this is precisely where we learn to uncover our own way of meeting the wisdom of the dharma. This is where dharma becomes integrated into our lives and path. This is where we learn what it means to practice the dharma. My teacher used to say, "It is one thing to want to practice dharma. It is an entirely different thing to know *how* to practice dharma." This practice of simmering and letting your self-importance have its pain is an essential point in the beginning, middle, and end.

If there were an easier way to reach our higher goal, we would try it, but there is no way around this if you want to be a dharma practitioner. Parents don't want to inflict pain on their children but recognize when they must go against their kids' desires to prevent them from being spoiled. Though it is initially painful for their children, wise parents do it anyway, knowing that this firm approach will spare them much greater suffering in the future, when they are out in the world on their own. In the same way, we need to be firm and uncompromising with our self-importance to reach our goal of freedom from its tyranny.

One of the mind training slogans is "Don't be a loyalist," but it is often translated as "Don't be so predictable." This means don't just follow the same old demands of your self-importance like a slave. Rid yourself of any obligation to feel loyal to your ego. Instead, do something new by simmering in the ego's pain, thus allowing your self-importance to reveal itself fully. Once you see it fully, you don't have to work hard to let it go. It releases its hold on you automatically.

When we appreciate how our training is causing us to grow, we develop a whole new attitude to the pain involved. This insight gives us the courage and confidence to go further and further with the training, allowing us to tolerate more and more severe blows to the ego. Our increasing strength gives us a stable feeling of well-being. Instead of feeling vulnerable to our own emotional reactions, we feel safe in our own mind. Instead of feeling threatened by the unpredictable, chaotic world we live in, waiting for the other shoe to drop, we feel relaxed, unthreatened, and at home in all situations.

This is the fruition of letting our self-importance have its pain: complete freedom from all mental and emotional disturbance and being comfortable in our own skin. Whenever we practice simmering, it has a tremendous effect, which gradually accumulates. Over time, there is less and less pain because there is less and less self-importance. This is how we achieve the peaceful heart.

102

I should not be irritated, saying,
"They are obstacles to my good deeds."
For is not patience the supreme austerity,
And should I not abide by this?

103

And if I fail to practice patience,
Hindered by my own shortcomings,
I myself create impediments
To merit's causes, yet so close at hand.

We may think that if someone threatens our wealth, belongings, status, or power—or hinders us from acquiring them—it will become more difficult to make offerings and perform other acts of generosity. Doesn't that justify protecting these things with aggression?

Yes, it's true that having fewer resources can make it harder to practice generosity, but there is something deeper to consider here as well. Wealth, status, power, beauty, influence, and all other positive conditions come as the fruit of past virtuous deeds. If we react with aggression to what seems to threaten these things, we can burn the positive seeds that have generated these desirable states.

Instead of burning our positive seeds, we can use apparent threats and obstacles to help us create new seeds of virtue. First, we should step back and reflect on cause and effect. We all have both positive and negative seeds that can ripen at any time given the right causes and conditions. When our past negative actions ripen and we perceive that our wealth, status, or plans to be generous are threatened, we can use these circumstances as an opportunity to work with our tendency to react aggressively. If we do so with the vision of bodhicitta, and if we practice patience with the clear intention to meet all hardships with love and compassion for the benefit of all beings, we can accumulate great waves of merit. Furthermore, if we dedicate these intentions and actions for the enlightenment of all beings, then our merit will become like the drop of water in the ocean that we spoke of earlier. Our merit will not be exhausted or burned up but will continue to support our path until we attain enlightenment.

So if merit is really our main concern, then we have no reason to complain when someone gets in the way of our initial plans to be generous, because in losing one opportunity for merit, we gain a much greater one. We should make sure not to waste such a chance by simply getting angry. This may be difficult to do all at once, but if we can contemplate the principle and come to understand the logic behind it, then slowly we will be able to rise to each occasion as it presents itself in our lives.

104

If something does not come to be when something
    else is absent,
And does arise, that factor being present,
That factor is indeed its cause.
How can it, then, be said to hinder it?

105

The beggars who arrive at proper times
Are not an obstacle to generosity.
We cannot say that those who give the vows
Are hindrances to ordination!

106

The beggars in this world are numerous;
Assailants are comparatively few.
For if I do no harm to others,
Others do no injury to me.

107

So, like a treasure found at home,
That I have gained without fatigue,
My enemies are helpers in my Bodhisattva work
And therefore they should be a joy to me.

108

Since I have grown in patience
Thanks to them,

To them its first fruits I should give,
For of my patience they have been the cause.

We tend to think of being provoked as an obstacle, not just in general but also to our Buddhist practice and path. We think our bodhisattva path would be smoother if we were free of irritating people or challenging circumstances. But Shantideva shows us that the opposite is the case. An effect can only arise in the presence of its cause. This is the very definition of cause and effect. For example, without anyone in need, there is no chance for us to practice generosity. To say that a beggar is an obstacle to generosity makes no sense. Similarly, if you want to become a monk or a nun, it's illogical to think of the person who ordains you as an obstacle to your vows.

Patience is the most essential skill to master if we are to develop a peaceful heart. Since the cause of patience is provocation, how can we say we're practicing patience when there is nothing to provoke us? With this reasoning, how can someone who disturbs us or obstructs our desires be a hindrance to the bodhisattva path? The only true hindrance is our own failure to recognize and then seize the opportunity by letting ourselves react habitually with aggression or retaliation, thinking things should be different than they are.

Because the world is full of people and other beings in need, we have unlimited ways and opportunities to be generous. But opportunities to practice patience become comparatively rare. This is due to karma, the law of cause and effect. When someone harms us, that is the result of our having harmed them at some point in the past. But as we begin to turn our minds away from self-interest and toward altruism and tsewa, we inflict less and less harm on others. The natural consequence is that there will be fewer and fewer beings harming and provoking us.

A traditional contemplation that helps us develop unbiased love is to think of all beings as "mother sentient beings." In each of your countless past lives, you had a mother. Every one of those mothers cared for you just like your mother in this life. Every mother fed you, protected you, taught you, worried about you, sacrificed for you. Every mother gave you kindness that you will never be able to repay. But now the vast majority of your kind mothers are lost in the realms of samsara, going through an endless succession of painful emotions and experiences, with no light of wisdom to help them see their way out. This is so for even the most harmful and threatening beings you've encountered in this life. They are all your dear mothers and all—with very few exceptions—are wandering in the darkness of ignorance. By generating universal compassion and love with such thoughts, we gradually change our karmic relationship with each being. It is said that when you appreciate someone as your mother, they start to see you as their child. Over time this becomes true of even the most vicious creatures and demonic forces. They respond to your compassion and become sensitive to your well-being.

The only "drawback" to having these improved relations with beings is that we don't have many chances to practice patience, one of the most essential practices for the aspiring bodhisattva. Therefore, when someone does provoke us, we should see it as a rare opportunity that we can't afford to pass up. It is also an unsolicited opportunity, for we are not going out looking for trouble. Thanks to some unresolved karma, the trouble has conveniently appeared at home or on the job without any exertion on our part. For bodhisattvas who are serious about practicing patience, this is like a wish-fulfilling jewel falling into their lap.

Gyalse Ngulchu Thogme, a Tibetan monk who lived in the fourteenth century, wrote the pithy *Thirty-Seven Practices of the Bodhisattva*, a distillation of Shantideva's *Way of the Bodhisattva*. Though he had no interest in material possessions, he received many offerings from his devoted students. Since it felt like a burden to keep these offerings, he would find ways to offer them again on behalf of the donors, dedicating the merit to their enlightenment.

Once he was traveling to Lhasa with the intention of making many offerings in front of the Jowo Rinpoche, the statue of Buddha Shakyamuni that is considered the most sacred image in Tibet. On the way there, a group of bandits attacked him. They not only robbed him, they beat him up. As they were departing, he noticed they had missed a huge nugget of turquoise in one of his deep pockets. So he called out, "Hey, come back! You forgot this!" When they returned, the leader said, "We robbed you and beat you up, and you want to give us your last turquoise? What kind of man are you?" Ngulchu Thogme said, "I feel grateful and relieved because of what you've done for me. I had these burdensome offerings for a long time and couldn't figure out what to do with them. Finally, I decided to bring them to Lhasa so I could make many feast and butter lamp offerings in front of the Jowo. But now that you've robbed me, I can go back to my hermitage and meditate. I don't have to go all the way to Lhasa anymore!"

The bandits were moved by what he said and felt tremendous remorse. They could see how much wisdom and compassion he had. They returned all his possessions and accompanied him to Lhasa, protecting and serving him along the way. When they got to the Jokhang, the temple housing the sacred statue, they helped him make the offerings. Ngulchu Thogme dedicated the merit not only to the original patrons but also to the bandits for inciting him to practice patience and for helping him exhaust his negative karma. This is a true story and a perfect illustration of how to benefit from "adverse" circumstances.

109
And if I say my foes should not be honored
Since they did not mean to stimulate my patience,
Why do I revere the Sacred Dharma,
Cause indeed of my attainment?

Being provoked is an indispensable part of developing a peaceful heart. This is the unconventional reasoning that Shantideva has expounded throughout the Patience Chapter. But at this point, you may say, "Yes, I understand your argument. But isn't it going too far to *honor* my aggressors and enemies? After all, they have no intention to benefit me. They have no positive intention whatsoever!"

Here Shantideva points out that the dharma in and of itself also has no actual intention to benefit us. The dharma consists of inanimate books made of inanimate words. These books do not think *I hope people read me because I want to make them enlightened.* They don't care if we read them or not. The reason we respect these books is because of their effect, not their intention. If we make proper use of the wisdom they contain, they will help us free ourselves from our attachment to the self, the root cause of all suffering. In the same way, if we make proper use of anyone's provoking behavior, we will also progress swiftly toward liberation from samsara.

110

"These enemies conspired to harm me," I protest,
"And therefore should receive no honors."
But had they worked to help me like a doctor,
How could I have brought forth patience?

111

Thanks to those whose minds are full of malice
I engender patience in myself.
They therefore are the causes of my patience,
Fit for veneration, like the Dharma.

We may agree with the reasoning that the dharma and those who provoke us are alike in that both help us without intending to. But then we may point out that, unlike the neutral dharma, people who harm us actually have a negative intention. How can we respect and appreciate anyone who is against our well-being?

Sometimes dharma and our worldly ways go together, but there are critical junctures where they diverge. This is an example of a clear divergence. Shantideva says that if we value opportunities to practice patience, which become increasingly hard to come by as we progress along the path, then we must value those who actively behave against our well-being. We are presented with a choice. We can go with the conventional ways of our culture, for which we will receive support from nearly everyone around us, including most of our family members and friends. Or we can try a different approach.

As we have seen, these teachings show that our patience practice completely depends on the animosity and provocation of others. Sometimes doctors inflict painful treatments on us, such as harsh medicine or surgery. But because their aim is to benefit us, they don't help us develop patience. We also appreciate doctors when they make us better, not when they have a positive intention but fail to help us, which also happens. What counts for us is not their motivation, but the result. Similarly, for the cultivation of a peaceful heart, we should appreciate our enemies and those who provoke us for the results they can bring us, putting aside the question of their motivation.

It is important to reiterate that Shantideva's logical arguments are not just empty games of mental manipulation. If we treat them as such, they will have no power to help us. But if we take this unconventional thinking seriously and work hard to integrate Shantideva's reasoning into our own, we will discover its tremendous potential to bring the mind out of its painful ruts of confusion and habitual reaction.

To become inspired enough to make such a change in our thinking and habits requires a measure of desperation with samsara. We may have to feel at the end of our rope to let go of our excuses and stubbornness and be ready to apply such radical methods for becoming unstuck. Without being inspired by some desperation, by a deeper level of pain, or by understanding what is at stake, it will be hard to penetrate the density of our habitual patterns.

This is a point that all practitioners have to reach for themselves. If people aren't ready, there's no point in saying, "Don't worry! This is good for you!" Such optimistic remarks can come across as condescending and judgmental. Instead of inspiring us to apply the unconventional approach of dharma, these comments tend to have the opposite effect. They can make us dig in our heels and strengthen our resolve to dwell in a state of intolerance and self-righteousness. Reacting with aggression is our default way of venting frustration and getting things off our chest. For that reason, it feels like a relief—even though that relief is short-lived and leads to a powerful backlash. But until we are ready to look objectively at the full story of aggression and what it does to us, it will feel like the natural, and even necessary, way to react.

Until we are so fed up with our habitual, self-destructive patterns that we decide to look for relief elsewhere—such as in the soothing wisdom of teachers like Shantideva—we will continue to pile suffering upon ourselves. It is heartening to think that humankind in Shantideva's eighth century had all the same habitual patterns of reactions and disturbing states of mind that we do, and that the dharma applies to us as much as it did to them.

Nonetheless, the conventional approach is what we see all around us, so it is hard to really believe that any other approach can work. It's helpful then to reflect on where conventional approaches have gotten humankind and our world and where the approach of dharma can lead us instead. Doing so will help us take these teachings more seriously. Then our progress will be swift.

It is said that when bodhisattvas from other realms look at our world, many of them want to live here. They see excellent opportunities to perfect the practices of bodhicitta and grow toward the full enlightenment of buddhahood. They may also feel a measure of apprehension because our world is so challenging. But for all the bodhisattvas who have taken birth here and thrived in this environment, the patience they have cultivated has been their greatest support. Patience gives bodhisattvas—and practitioners of all levels—the means to continue in samsara without drowning in it. It allows us to be like the beautiful lotus that grows out of the muddy water but floats pristinely on the surface. The flower's nourishment comes from and is directly connected to the mud, yet it blossoms above the muddy water. This is a profound and beautiful analogy for the bodhisattva path.

These stanzas mark the end of the longest section of the Patience Chapter, in which Shantideva teaches us how to work with the many types of yi midewe ze, the food that disturbs the mind. From here, he shifts his emphasis to the reasons why we should respect all sentient beings.

ELEVEN

We Can't Attain Enlightenment without Sentient Beings

112

And so the mighty Sage has spoken of the field of beings
As well as of the field of Conquerors.
Many who brought happiness to beings,
Have passed beyond, attaining perfection.

113

Thus the state of Buddhahood depends
On beings and on buddhas equally.
What kind of practice is it then
That honors only buddhas but not beings?

To progress along the spiritual path, we have to plant seeds and cultivate our crop in two fields: the field of awakened beings and the field of sentient beings. Every step of the way, we need both fields equally. The awakened beings—buddhas and bodhisattvas—teach us, guide us, protect us, inspire us, and serve as examples. It is obvious why these magnificent people merit our respect.

But sentient beings—those who are still caught in the suffering of samsara—are just as important for our progress toward enlightenment and therefore merit tremendous respect as well. Such respect and appreciation, however, doesn't come naturally to our minds. It is far from automatic for us to revere those who exhibit the same confusion and neuroses that we have. Therefore, Shantideva sets out to explain how to make this shift in perspective, which is so profound and critical for the path.

Respect for all sentient beings is not some groundless, idealistic sentiment. The need for such respect is based on clear intelligence. This intelligence comes from reviewing our lives objectively and taking note of two basic things: what has always helped us and what has always harmed us.

What has helped you the most, not only in this life but in all your lifetimes in samsara? Your fellow sentient beings. Before you were conceived, you were a disembodied consciousness roaming around in search of a body to call home. Your mother and father, through the gift of their egg and sperm, gave your consciousness a stable place to enter and in which to dwell. Then your mother lent you her womb for nine months so you could develop all the parts of your new body and reach the stage where you were ready to come out into the world. This wasn't easy for her. Every month, you became heavier and more uncomfortable to carry, and the act of giving birth, wonderful though it may have been, was also extremely painful and full of fear and danger. Then, once you were born, your mother and the other important people in your life cared for you with continual kindness, making sure you had everything you needed to grow up into the fine adult you are today. Without the kindness of your parents, teachers, mentors, friends, and many others, you would not even have your basic human abilities and values, let alone the most precious ability to follow the path to enlightenment.

Over the course of our countless lifetimes in samsara, the care, compassion, and generosity we've received from others has been infinite. Every positive moment we've experienced has been the result of the kindness of others. And it is not that only some beings have been kind to us while others have always been unkind. Because the complex and malleable nature of karma is always changing the character of our relationships, no one is intrinsically kind or unkind. As Tai Situ Rinpoche, one of the great Tibetan Buddhist teachers living today, has said, "Everyone has been your mother, your father, your sister, your brother, your friend, your enemy, your breakfast, your lunch."

This means that every living being has at some time been crucial to our happiness and well-being. If we reflect on our history in samsara from this point of view, we will have a firm basis to be grateful to everyone. Of course, we could take the opposite tack and focus on the pain that each being has inflicted on us, but the point of this reflection—and all Buddhist practice—is to open our hearts. As mentioned earlier, when beings have inflicted pain on us, we can reflect on how those who harm us have also helped bring us to where we are now. They have done so by bringing things to the point where we need to seek a different way of relating to our circumstances and more generally by exposing to us the painful nature of samsara.

The second part of this contemplation is to think about what has always been unfavorable to us. We can blame all the difficulties in our lives on many things—outer circumstances, people, our emotions, our thought patterns—but these have all come from one cause, which, as I've been saying throughout this book, is the exclusively self-centered mind. Our attachment to this self is the root of all the seventy-two ways we get disturbed. Thus, it is the cause of all our harmful thoughts, words, and actions, which in turn have created all the negative karma we keep having to endure. All the pain of samsara comes from the sticky relationship we each have with the illusory self—this self that we feel exists but we can never find, no matter how hard we look. I keep returning to this from many different angles because this essential point is often overlooked. As simple as it is to say, letting knowledge truly sink in takes time and repetition, repeatedly examining how this is so in your own experience.

Now, the irony is that we cling to this sticky relationship even though its unpleasantness haunts us day and night. For example, we may see another human being in a desperate situation. We have a tinge of compassion and desire to help, but then fear or tightness gets in the way. Instead of helping, we contract and take refuge in our excuses. Does anyone enjoy that feeling of tightness or contraction inside? Does anyone want to be stuck with that inability to act from a tender heart? Do we really enjoy turning away? I don't think so. But as long as we are under the power of ego—of our exclusively self-centered mind-set—we have no freedom to do otherwise.

One of the mind training slogans is "All dharma agrees at a single point." This means that all our efforts to study and practice should be aimed at first recognizing, then reducing, and ultimately letting go of our attachment to the self. This aim, however, must be free from self-hatred and self-aggression, which, as I have mentioned, are merely self-centered mind in a different guise. Instead, we should motivate ourselves by thinking objectively about the ego, about what it has done to us and what it will keep doing to us in the future if left unchecked. Motivated by critical intelligence—as opposed to emotional reactivity—we can gradually become less gullible and less susceptible to the charms and tricks of our self-cherishing mind. Then we will feel the same way about the ego that we feel about a false friend who has been deceiving us. Our discovery of the betrayal naturally squashes the affection we had for that friend. In the same way, our realization of the pitfalls of self-centered mind will naturally dissolve our affection for our attachment to the self.

This attachment will still arise, but we will begin to see through the charade. We will become more and more like an old man watching children play a game, which is a traditional analogy. No matter how seriously the children take their game, the old man never buys into it. He observes the scene in a state of amusement and kindly humor. In the same way, when self-centered thoughts and emotions occur in our minds, instead of taking them seriously and reacting to them with grasping or rejection, we can simply let them arise and dissolve naturally, also in a state of amusement and kindly humor.

In your mind stream, only one thought can appear at a time. Thoughts can happen quickly one after another, but you can never think two thoughts at once. It may seem like you can, but if you slow down enough and observe, you will soon find it is impossible to have a thought about yourself and someone else at the same time.

Our unconscious samsaric habit is to focus our attention exclusively on this self, but as we come to understand the perils of self-centered mind, we can replace these thoughts with more and more consideration for others. We can put ourselves in others' shoes. Then, as the proportions gradually shift toward altruistic thinking, we will enjoy increasing freedom from the tyranny of an egocentric stance. Thinking altruistically of others 10 percent of the time is 10 percent freedom from disturbed mind. Twenty percent of our thoughts devoted to others is 20 percent freedom. There is no reason to stop at any level; we can keep going until our entire attention is wholeheartedly devoted to the welfare of others.

Here it is helpful to remember that when we care for others, we are naturally caring for ourselves as well. There is no need to create an artificial separation between "me" and "you." As our own hearts open and our actions toward others become imbued with tsewa, our own needs are taken care of naturally. As we continue to progress in this way, our minds will become less fearful, irritable, stubborn, and confused. We will become more loving, courageous, flexible, and joyful. This is the result of switching our allegiance from self-interest to care for others.

There is one important point to clarify about this transfer of allegiance. Focusing on others must include close friends and family members—those for whom affection comes easily. But you will make no progress in overcoming self-clinging if you see these people as members of your ego's empire. Then your care for "others" will just become more yi midewe ze, more food to disturb your heart and mind.

It is important to remember that many of the ways we get disturbed come from seeing others as extensions of ourselves. According to the traditional classification, twenty-four of the seventy-two causes of mental indigestion are related to our attachment to people we consider to be "mine." For example, your mind is disturbed by attachment not only when you desire praise but also when your child desires praise. It is disturbed by aversion not only when you are insulted but also when your good friend is insulted.

But when you think about the ones you love, try to remember that they are individual sentient beings with their own karma. Before your children came into your life, you didn't have any special feelings toward them. Nor will you have such feelings after you depart this life and are reborn in a completely new situation with new relationships. Your strong bond with your family members and dear friends is the result of karma ripening in this lifetime. It is wonderful to have these bonds with others. They open your heart and provide a powerful medium for tsewa to flow freely and exuberantly. But at the same time, we must take care that the key point of our dharma practice—becoming free from attachment to the self—is not hijacked by thoughts of *my* child, *my* spouse, *my* dear friend, *me, me, ME!*

114
Not in the qualities of their minds
But in the fruits they give are they alike.
In beings, too, such excellence resides,
And therefore beings and buddhas are the same.

The kind buddhas have the intention to bring us onto the path and then guide us to the state of enlightenment. Sentient beings don't have that intention. Even among those beings who care for us the most, very few, if any, have a vision for our enlightenment. In this way, buddhas and beings are not alike.

But whether they have the intention or not, beings are equally important to our progress along the path. They can benefit us in ways that the buddhas cannot. For example, because buddhas lack nothing, they don't need our generosity. Because they are free from samsara, they are not proper objects of our compassion. And because we don't rub skins and clash with them, they don't provoke us and don't give us any opportunities to practice patience.

If we think of sentient beings as emissaries of the buddhas, we will appreciate their tremendous potential to help us along the bodhisattva path. We venerate the buddhas not because of what they symbolize but because of what they can do to transform our minds and change our lives. Since sentient beings have an equally large role in this process, Shantideva says we should venerate them equally.

Another reason to place sentient beings on the same level as buddhas is that they are identical in their ultimate nature. The only thing that separates us from the buddhas is our ignorance. Because we see ourselves and our world as intrinsically existent, we are constantly caught up in cherishing and protecting the self. But as we have seen, this self is a product of ignorance. When we take the time to look for an intrinsic self, we are unable to pinpoint anything as "me."

This ignorance is not who we are. It is adventitious, like clouds that veil the sky. Who we truly are is like the pristine blue sky. Our deepest nature is just like the mind and heart of all the buddhas—wise beyond measure and infinitely flowing with tsewa. On an overcast day, we may notice the clouds more than the sky, but the sky is always present, unstained, and ready to reveal itself.

This is true for you and me and every other sentient being. By applying the Buddha's teachings, every one of us can eventually become enlightened. Focusing on this potential, rather than on the temporary confusion that veils our nature, gives us another basis for respecting beings as much as buddhas.

115
Offerings made to those with loving minds
Reveal the eminence of living beings.
Merit that accrues from faith in Buddha
Shows in turn the Buddha's eminence.

Buddhas and beings are both eminent because of their capacity to purify our minds and help us accumulate merit. The first part of this stanza is illustrated by a traditional story. Once a mother and daughter were holding hands as they crossed a wide river. The current became too powerful and separated them, sweeping them both downstream. The mother thought, *I don't care what happens to me as long as my daughter is safe.* The daughter had the same loving thoughts about her mother. Both of them died and were reborn in a celestial realm. Neither of them had been practitioners in their lives, but the merit of their final altruistic thoughts was enough to bring about such a positive result. Their selfless love was only possible because they had each other as objects of that love. As this story illustrates, without sentient beings in our lives, our tsewa could remain dormant forever; with them, it has abundant chances to flow. If we cultivate it with wisdom, it can expand immeasurably.

In relation to the Buddha and other enlightened beings, we accumulate merit and purify our ignorance through faith. For example, the act of setting up a shrine and offering bowls of fresh water every day opens us to the vast mind of the buddhas and bodhisattvas, which is inseparable from our own innate nature. For countless eons, they have gathered inexhaustible merit and dedicated every drop to the enlightenment of all sentient beings. But unless we make a connection to them, we can't receive the benefit of their altruistic actions. Making offerings is one of the most powerful ways of creating and deepening such a connection. In this way, we get to take part in their immeasurable merit, which we can then dedicate for the greatest benefit of all and for our own path to enlightenment.

116

Although not one of them is equal
To the buddhas, who are oceans of perfection,
Because they have a share in bringing forth enlightenment,
Beings may be likened to the buddhas.

117

If of such a gathering of supreme excellence
A tiny part appeared in certain beings,
The three worlds made in offering to them
Would be a very little thing.

118
Since there lies in beings a share
In bringing forth the supreme and enlightened state,
By virtue of this parity alone
It's right that I should reverence them.

In terms of their qualities, buddhas and sentient beings are quite different. A buddha is completely free of ignorance and has developed unsurpassable wisdom, tsewa, and power to benefit others. Sentient beings are caught in the suffering of samsara. Most of us can hardly benefit ourselves, let alone others. However, Shantideva reiterates, buddhas and beings are equally important for our progress toward enlightenment. And since enlightenment is the most significant thing in the universe, anyone who plays even the tiniest role in bringing about such a result is worthy of tremendous respect.

TWELVE

Our Kindness Delights the Buddhas

119

The buddhas are my true, unfailing friends.
Boundless are the benefits they bring to me.
How else may I repay their goodness
But by making living beings happy?

There is nothing you can do to make the buddhas and bodhi-sattvas happier than being kind and compassionate to sentient beings. Other than their wish to benefit beings, they have no needs or desires of their own. In their deep wisdom mind, they are always aware of our suffering. They see our ignorance and how it continu-ally brings about disturbing emotions that manifest outwardly as our realms of samsara. They see how deprived we are of the peace and joy that are innately part of our enlightened—but obscured—nature. The buddhas and bodhisattvas have no ulterior motives. They are free from the self-cherishing and craving that torment us. *If you give me this or do this to please me, I'll be happy. But if you don't, I'll be very unhappy and will punish you.* Such thoughts don't run through their minds because their only aim is to bring benefit to beings.

It is said that for a buddha, not even the smallest act—not even the blink of an eye—is without purpose. That purpose is to help sentient beings transform their own minds. It is also said that bud-dhas never miss a chance to benefit beings. The only factor that determines whether they can help us is our own openness. Because the buddhas have completely overcome the misunderstanding of a boundary between self and other, their minds are limitless and all-pervasive. They don't have to come from a distant universe. They are always with us, fully ready and willing to help us free ourselves from samsara. There are many ways in which we can position ourselves to receive their wisdom and compassion. Saying prayers or even thinking about them is enough to create the necessary openness. But the greatest way of receiving the aid of enlightened beings is for us to be loving to others.

This is illustrated by the story of Asanga and his quest to meet the Buddha Maitreya. Asanga isolated himself in strict retreat, devoting all his time to practices related to Maitreya. His hope was for Maitreya to appear before him and give him instructions that would lead him to enlightenment. But after six years of diligent practice with no results, Asanga got frustrated and left. On his way home, he met a man who was rubbing a large iron bar with a soft piece of cloth. When Asanga asked what he was doing, the man said he was making a needle. Amazed at the effort people go through to accomplish futile aims, Asanga realized he needed to be more persistent on his path to enlightenment. So he returned to his retreat, determined never to give up. But three years later, when Maitreya still hadn't appeared, not even in a dream, Asanga again left. This time he met a man who was stroking a massive boulder with a feather dipped in water. The man told him that he wanted to wear away the boulder because it was blocking the sunlight from his house. This gave Asanga renewed determination to keep persevering with his practice. But still Maitreya didn't come.

Another uneventful and discouraging three years passed. Finally, Asanga left again and began to wander around, feeling hopeless and lost. He saw a crippled dog dragging herself along the road. Her rotting body was infested with maggots that were eating her flesh. Full of pain and aggression, the dog barked viciously at Asanga when he came closer. The sight broke Asanga's heart. He thought about how to remove the maggots. If he used his hands, the maggots would probably be crushed, so the only way was to use his tongue. Disgusted by the rotting flesh, Asanga closed his eyes and stretched out to lick the maggots out of the dog. But as far as he stretched, he still didn't feel the maggots. Finally, he felt his tongue touch the ground. He opened his eyes. Instead of the dog, Maitreya stood before him.

"How little compassion you have!" Asanga burst out. "I practiced for twelve years, and you didn't even appear in my dreams!" Maitreya said, "Since the very first day of your retreat, I've been right there with you, but you didn't have the openness to see me. Your twelve years of practice made your obscurations thinner. Today, your pure compassion for this dog finally made you open enough to see me in person. If you don't believe me, put me on your shoulder and walk around." Asanga put Maitreya on his shoulder and walked around at a fair, asking people what they saw on his shoulder. No one saw anything. They just thought he was crazy. Finally, an old woman, who also had developed enough openness to have higher perceptions, asked, "Why are you carrying a rotten dog on your shoulder?"

120

By helping beings we repay the ones
Who sacrifice their lives for us and plunge into the hell of
    Unrelenting Pain.
Should beings therefore do great harm to me,
I'll strive to bring them only benefit.

121

For those who have become my lords,
At times, took care not even of their bodies.
Why should I, a fool, behave with such conceit?
Why should I not become the slave of others?

If a buddha has a chance to go to the pit of hell and feel its burning fire in order to benefit even the tiniest sentient being, there would be no hesitation whatsoever. For example, Avalokiteshvara, known as the embodiment of compassion, is said to visit the hell realms three times every day to help whoever he can. This level of courage is the fruit of having completely realized that there is no self to cherish and protect.

It is not the case, however, that the buddhas can simply wipe away our karma and take us to a pure realm where there is no suffering. We all have to purify our own karma and travel our own path to wake up to our enlightened nature. But the buddhas do everything in their power to help us, never holding back and never missing a chance. Such is the immensity of their love and care for all of us.

If we truly honor and respect enlightened beings for all they do, then the best way to show our gratitude is by joining their effort to benefit others and practicing patience whenever beings provoke or harm us. This is the only way to repay them for all the kindness they have shown us, mainly in the form of the teachings that have touched us and brought increasing peace and joy into our lives.

Our efforts to benefit others, furthermore, should not come with an air of superiority but with an attitude of humility. If we are not careful, it is easy for egotistical or self-centered tendencies, such as pride and desire for recognition or power, to taint our motivation. Therefore, instead of seeing ourselves as lords of sentient beings, we should see ourselves as their servants. The mind-set of the bodhisattva is to think at all times of how we can serve other beings, whoever they are. We have many opportunities to serve those who are close to us, as long we don't see them as mere extensions of ourselves. From there, we can extend our love further and further out, until we realize the limitless potential of our innate heart of tsewa.

122
Buddhas are made happy by the joy of beings.
They sorrow, they lament when beings suffer.
By bringing joy to beings, then, I please the buddhas also;
By wounding them, I wound the buddhas too.

123

Just as there's no sensual delight
To please the mind of one whose body burns in fire,
There is no way to please the great compassionate ones
While we ourselves are causes of another's pain.

124

The damage I have done to beings
Saddens all the buddhas in their great compassion.
Therefore, all these evils I confess today
And pray that they will bear with my offences.

How we treat children has a big effect on their mothers. When we are kind to children and make them happy, it makes their mothers even happier. But when we make a child suffer, the mother feels even more pain than the child. Since this is just how the buddhas feel about each and every sentient being, we must take tremendous care to treat all beings well.

If we are careless in this regard, there will be no connection between us and the buddhas. No offerings, praises, or prayers will have the effect we want if we cause beings pain. It would be like pouring kerosene on somebody, setting them on fire, and then bringing them the most delicious food and brilliant entertainment. Who could enjoy anything with their body on fire? This is why there is no merit in animal sacrifices and other harmful rites that may appear to have a good cause. Any noble being worthy of our veneration would not be won over by an action that causes such distress to others.

When we understand the buddhas' deep love for beings, we will realize how displeased it makes them to see beings harmed. If we realize we have caused others harm, at this point, we can either sink into guilt or admit our wrongdoings and leave them behind. Succumbing to guilt will only make us identify more closely with the one who committed those actions. This means that instead of learning from our mistakes and resolving not to fall prey to such delusion again, we lean toward identifying more closely with our ignorance. We think the ignorance is more who we are than our intention to learn and do better in the future.

This is a very important distinction. If we identify with our ignorance, we won't learn anything, and we won't change. Therefore, we will be much better off if we recognize that the ignorance at the root of all our harmful actions is a universal affliction among all beings in samsara. Before we couldn't help being ignorant; we couldn't know what we didn't know. Now, however, thanks to the light of dharma, we can see our thoughts and actions more clearly, and we can do better. Our only productive course is to admit our past behavior and then to move on, applying the teachings on patience.

125
That I might rejoice the buddhas' hearts,
Henceforth I will be master of myself, the servant of
    the world.
I shall not seek revenge though crowds may trample
    on my head or kill me.
Let the Guardians of the world rejoice!

If you followed a committed proponent of nonviolence such as Mahatma Gandhi, you would know that taking up arms against your enemies would displease him more than anything else you could do. His nonviolent vision was what inspired millions of Indians to use civil disobedience rather than weapons in their struggle against the British Raj. When they did resort to physical attacks, Gandhi went on hunger strike to get them to stop. He thought there was no purpose in going on as a leader if his followers committed violence. If we see the buddhas and bodhisattvas as our leaders, we should be similarly dedicated to avoiding aggression against sentient beings.

To practice nonviolence successfully, it is important to work with one's pride. An inflated self-image gets in the way of tolerating the harmful behavior of others. Great practitioners from many noble spiritual traditions purposely cultivate the view that they are the lowest of the low. This is not because of a lack of self-esteem, for they have total confidence in their own enlightened nature. But taking the low position gives them a mental ease and flexibility that's unavailable when one tries to maintain one's supposed position with comparative and competitive mind.

Patrul Rinpoche, whose oral teachings on *The Way of the Bodhisattva* were written down later as *The Nectar of Manjushri's Speech*, wrote a letter to himself that contained advice on this practice of humility. He said that compared to him, there were many people with far greater talents. Many people were far superior in conducting both worldly and spiritual affairs. But recognizing this disparity did not make him feel bad about himself. Instead, it liberated him from any temptations to compete with others or to prove himself in any way. Such a mind-set left him free and easy to serve others selflessly, without any hope for reward or even good treatment. It gave him the strength not to retaliate when he was harmed.

Jesus told his followers to "turn the other cheek." This mentality requires much greater strength than the Mafia mentality, where the default course of action is revenge—the principle of an eye for an eye. Witnessing such tolerance is highly gratifying to the buddhas and bodhisattvas. They are not happy because you've been abused but because you've stopped recreating the karma that keeps yourself and others stuck in the otherwise endless cycle of samsara. If one person helps stop the perpetuation of violence among beings, that is a great victory for the entire world.

126
The great compassionate lords consider as themselves
All beings—there's no doubt of this.
Those whom I perceive as beings are buddhas in themselves;
How can I not treat them with respect?

In the early stages of his path, the Buddha considered all his elders to be his parents, all people his age to be his brothers and sisters, and all those younger than him to be his children. Later he meditated on the equality of self and other, which the eighth chapter of *The Way of the Bodhisattva* explains in detail. The aim of this practice is to see how all beings are exactly like ourselves in their innate wish to be happy and free from suffering. Because we have so much care for ourselves, when we fully realize this equality, we will feel just as much care for all other sentient beings.

Since it may sound impossible to have such deep concern for the limitless beings throughout space, Shantideva suggests that we reflect on how many parts our body contains. That number is also limitless, yet we protect and care for every single part because all are included in "my body." In the same way, we can train our minds to think of all beings as part of our self—not the small self we habitually cling to, but a big, universal self that encompasses all who desire happiness and freedom from pain, which is every living being without exception.

When we attain enlightenment, the distinction and duality between self and other will be completely eliminated, and we will no longer need to apply conceptual effort to consider other beings as ourselves. At that time, we will directly see the true nature of all beings, which is also our own nature. This is the innate enlightened nature that is now temporarily obscured by ignorance as the sun is temporarily obscured by clouds.

127

This very thing is pleasing to the buddhas' hearts
And perfectly secures the welfare of myself.
This will drive away the sorrows of the world,
And therefore it will be my constant work.

As we have seen, our kindness to other beings is what pleases buddhas the most. It also secures our own welfare because it ensures that we accumulate merit and purify negativity. If we respect sentient beings as we respect the buddhas, we will have more strength to practice patience when they harm us. Not retaliating when we are harmed is the beginning of changing our negative karma to positive karma. It also puts an end to the cycle of inflicting and receiving pain that has been going on for perhaps many lifetimes. If we keep practicing in this way, we will gradually gain the courage and limitless heart of the bodhisattvas, who always help the ones who harm them. Even if there's nothing they can do at the moment, they still have the intention to benefit the wrongdoer in the future. This turns what would normally be a negative connection into a positive one.

The result of this gradual shift in our minds and actions is that all the good things in the world start coming to us naturally, whether we want them or not. Our intention is to benefit others, but without making any self-directed effort, our merit brings us tremendous benefit as well. The traditional analogy relates to crops and their by-products. When you plant barley seeds, your intention is to reap a harvest of barley, and you work on this goal diligently. But without any special motivation, you also end up with an abundance of hay. If we use these positive life circumstances to enable our dharma practice to flourish, we will eventually attain enlightenment and be able to drive away the countless sorrows of beings, day after day, year after year, eon after eon, with the motivation that all beings become completely free from the sufferings of samsara.

THIRTEEN

The Karmic Consequences
of How We Treat Others

128
Imagine that the steward of a king
Does injury to multitudes of people.
Those with clear, farseeing eyes
Do not respond with violence even if they can.

129
For stewards, after all, are not alone.
They are supported by the kingly power.
Therefore I will not despise
The feeble beings tormenting me.

130
Their allies are the guardians of hell
And also the compassionate buddhas.
Therefore living beings I will gratify
As subjects might placate a wrathful king.

We should treat someone who provokes us as we would treat a rude tax collector who comes for an audit. He wears a blue suit, a white shirt, and a black tie, and his hair is cut very short. He treats you with scorn even before he knows whether you owe money on back taxes. You would like to treat him with equal rudeness and shut the door in his face, but you know you're dealing with much more than this one man. You are actually dealing with the whole government and its awesome power to punish you. If you force him to leave or even talk back to him, something much more unpleasant may happen to you. So you have no alternative but to smile and serve him tea.

Every sentient being we encounter has the support and backing of the buddhas, who love all beings as a mother loves her only child. But it is not the loving buddhas who will come after us. It is our own karma. Many people who are considered intelligent fail to pay attention to cause and effect. But if they think their actions have no consequences, they will ruin the fruits of whatever efforts they make in life. How many people build up successful careers and gain great fame only to have their whole world collapse because they've tried to get away with corrupt behavior or abuse of power?

"Intelligence" is full of holes unless it takes into account effects that will manifest far into the future, even in future lives. This requires going beyond our direct perceptions and using our ability to make inferences. For example, you may have a platinum credit card and the temporary ability to buy anything you want. This may give you and others the impression that you are a master of the universe. But if you act like a fool and continually spend beyond your means, you will soon have the mark of bankruptcy stamped on your forehead.

On the other hand, if we always remember karma, the law of cause and effect, and act accordingly, we can feel secure about the future even if doesn't come up immediately like a bright sun. Every action based on tsewa is a solid investment in our future well-being. Every time we practice patience instead of giving in to aggression, we sow seeds for a stable, peaceful heart. The more we observe karma, the more instinctually we adopt positive behavior, which automatically brings us and others around us supportive and positive circumstances.

A friend of mine once said that if we could look back to see the three lifetimes before this one and look ahead to see our next three, we would act very differently. This idea goes with the saying: "If you want to know where you've come from, look at your current circumstances. If you want to know where you're going, examine your current deeds." Such words of wisdom encourage us to examine our thoughts and actions to abide by the natural law of cause and effect. By doing so, we can become genuinely intelligent people and eventually supremely wise bodhisattvas.

131

And yet, the pains of hell to be endured
Through making living beings suffer—
Could these ever be unleashed on me
By all the ire of such a king?

132

And even if that king were pleased,
Enlightenment he could not give to me.
For this will only be achieved
By bringing happiness to beings.

Say you do choose to shut the door on the tax collector. What's the worst thing that can happen to you? Perhaps some jail time and loss of wealth or reputation. It's highly unlikely that you'll be executed or tortured for tax evasion. Even if you defy the most ruthless tyrant to his face, the amount of harm he can do you is limited to this life alone. But if you act out of anger and cause harm to other sentient beings, you will sow seeds of karma that will ripen into painful experiences, now and far into the future, including your rebirths. For example, a chicken on a factory farm spends its entire life trapped in a tiny space, surrounded by endless noise, light, and the distress and aggression of other terrified chickens. It has no future other than to have its head chopped off when it is big enough. With rare exceptions, no tyrant can cause you as much as suffering as the average chicken endures. Nothing we go through in this life could compare to the sufferings of the lower realms. Think well on this.

At the other end of the spectrum, if you pay all your taxes or please the leader of your country, what is the best thing that can happen to you as a result? Even winning over the ruler of a continent would only get you some temporary comfort and a feeling of proximity to power. But by mastering your own mind and overcoming all your yi midewe ze, you will accumulate tremendous merit and purify all your negative deeds from the past. The ultimate result of this is the highest level of freedom and happiness: your own enlightenment for the benefit of all beings. This is the kind of perspective Shantideva is trying to show us that patience practice can give.

133

No need to mention future Buddhahood,
Achieved through bringing happiness to beings.
How can I not see that glory, fame, and pleasure
Even in this life will likewise come?

134

For patience in samsara brings such things
As beauty, health, and good renown.
Its fruit is great longevity,
The vast contentment of a universal king.

Shantideva concludes the Patience Chapter by speaking of some of the temporal benefits of patience. While still in samsara, we will enjoy physical and mental health, an abundance of positive energy, and a sense of authentic presence that is attractive to others. Our natural goodness will radiate from our being, which will magnetize wealth, renown, and good friends and family. We will live long lives without obstacles and pass from life to life without fear and anxiety. We will be able to accomplish great deeds for the benefit of others. We will enjoy the glory and well-being of a virtuous, powerful monarch.

All of this will come to us without our striving for it through self-cherishing and self-protection. It will be the natural result of cultivating tolerance and practicing patience as explained throughout this book. In other words, our temporal good fortune will not be the result of pursuing the eight worldly concerns.

Of course, none of these temporal outcomes of mastering patience come anywhere near the significance of enlightenment. If we think of these relative benefits as ultimate goals, we will be selling ourselves short. Nonetheless, these karmic effects are still meaningful to us worldly beings. They are the kinds of results that make people, including ourselves, say, "Wow!"

As you apply these teachings on patience, it is important to pay attention to their benefits, not just over long periods but also as you see them unfolding. If you handle one instance of getting disturbed successfully—if you manage to experience the unpleasant ripening of one karmic seed without reacting with aggression—you should take a moment to acknowledge this small accomplishment. What is the state of your heart and mind compared to when you initially felt disturbed? How does that compare to when you don't practice patience and instead give in to habitual patterns, which inevitably leads to mindlessly harming yourself and others? It may seem like a small moment, but this is actually a significant intersection. Instead of taking us toward ignorance, darkness, and confusion, our choice takes us in the opposite direction: toward peace, freedom, and confidence. We should notice and appreciate this great difference.

The wisdom and skillful means of patience give us the ability to maintain our well-being in all situations. We become independent of the myriad causes and conditions that continually threaten us. This independence frees us of the insecurity we have in relation to our mind, the insecurity that our intolerance may at any time be triggered and create a big mess. Unless we have practiced patience in depth and under a wide variety of circumstances, we all have some degree of this insecurity, from subtle to gross. Not only is this self-doubt unpleasant, but it also undermines our other good qualities. We all have many positive attributes, such as love, compassion, intelligence, wisdom, faith, generosity, and diligence, but we can't feel fully confident in them if we are shaky in our practice of patience. We all have tsewa in our hearts, but we can't express it freely while going through the continually disruptive drama of our irritations and disturbances. It is like being a young heir to a throne who has the potential to be a great ruler but still lacks the necessary maturity to be effective in that role.

As we slowly overcome our aggression through self-reflection and the skillful means of patience practice, as our minds and hearts grow more and more peaceful, it becomes possible for us to claim our other good qualities with confidence. From deep within ourselves, we will feel that there are no longer any obstacles to making great strides forward on the spiritual path. Right now, many teachings probably seem unrealistic or impossible for us to live up to. There may seem to be an infinite gap between our own abilities and the abilities of the great sages. But our lack of self-confidence is due in large part to our inability to trust our own minds because of their unpredictable reactiveness. Deep in our hearts, we harbor doubt as to whether we have the courage and resilience to overcome our ignorance completely and then turn all our efforts to caring for the countless beings in samsara.

Once we master patience, however, we will trust the stability of our mind and know we can rely on it in all circumstances. This self-confidence will help us bridge the gap between where we are and where we have the potential to be. Following and completing the path to enlightenment will then seem like a realistic possibility. We will see all the teachings and practices clearly before us, at our fingertips. This will give us a sense of being born again—"born-again bodhisattvas." All this can come about through the practices set out by Shantideva and other bodhisattvas who have graced our world.

As we continue to practice patience, our reasons for doing something so demanding will become increasingly apparent. We may currently be driven, at least in part, by the desire to be a "good person" or to improve ourselves on some level. While this is not a bad motivation, it is somewhat artificial because it comes out of a limited and conventional idea of what a good person is. Our faith in the practice is unstable because it is partly based on hearsay and conceptual notions rather than on direct experience. But as we taste the unmistakable peace and freedom that comes from recognizing and working with yi midewe ze, we will know the benefits of patience firsthand. This will encourage us to persevere in the practice until we reach its fruition.

We can't directly perceive the mastery of patience in others, but with many people we can infer it from outer signs. We can see in their demeanor a tremendous resolve. Modern paragons of patience such as His Holiness the Dalai Lama; Martin Luther King, Jr.; Mother Teresa; Leymah Gbowee; and many, many others who are less well known have shown themselves to be profoundly resolved individuals. They have no doubt about what state of mind they would like to have and what state they would like not to have. They have complete conviction that a heart free from aggression will best serve themselves and others. The confidence that comes from such a decisive mind has made them imperturbable in the face of challenges that would send most people into a state of deep frustration and despair. They were able to attain that level of resolve only by self-reflecting deeply and working step-by-step with the habitual tendency to react, blame, and lash out. Such an accomplishment didn't happen overnight. They first had to contemplate and understand what they'd be able to achieve through tolerance, and from there they slowly built the kind of strength that could change their world—and the world as a whole.

These examples of nonviolence show why patience is referred to as the most excellent "armor." Soldiers always wear some form of armor to protect themselves in battle. Insects have exoskeletons that prevent them from being easily crushed. But no outer armor can protect us from what disturbs us and tears us up inside. When it comes to our own painful and stuck states of mind and emotions, there is no physical way to protect ourselves. Nor is there anywhere to hide. The only armor that can safeguard us from the continual disturbances, confusions, and reactions that keep all sentient beings trapped in the misery of samsara is genuine patience. An old Chinese saying I once saw on the back of a box of tea sums things up well: "Those who know patience, know peace."

If you are shivering in an Alaskan blizzard and have no protection from the elements, you may fantasize about going to a tropical island where you can lie on the white sand and soak up the sun while gazing at the beautiful ocean. Wouldn't that change be a tremendous relief? All your tensions would melt away, and you would feel rejuvenated in your body, mind, and soul. The suffering most of us experience from anger and aggression is a hundred times worse than that of a freezing winter environment. If you come to realize this for yourself, you will similarly long to go to a place of ease and rejuvenation. Such a place exists in your own peaceful heart. All you need to get there is an effective mode of transportation. That transportation is none other than the practice of patience.

With this, I conclude my words on the Patience Chapter. I have taken the time to give this lengthy commentary because I feel there is nothing more important than having a genuinely peaceful heart, from which our innate tsewa can then radiate exuberantly and effortlessly. I also feel there is no deeper, more comprehensive work on this subject than Shantideva's chapter. Its 134 stanzas uncover the rich and subtle points that can change our lives profoundly if we stop to contemplate them, take them to heart, and apply them until they become second nature. These teachings from the eighth century have been studied and practiced by countless bodhisattvas of the past and still retain their full vitality as living wisdom. His Holiness the Dalai Lama has credited Shantideva for teaching him all he knows about compassion and tolerance, especially in the face of great challenges and injustice. I think many of today's great teachers would say something similar.

My hope is that practitioners will continue to find guidance and inspiration in these teachings and develop a passion for self-reflection and for working with the ego and the seventy-two ways we get disturbed. This passion will enrich our lives and make every day of our existence deeply productive and meaningful.

When I was a young monk in India, I loved going to the bazaar. One day my old tutor said to me, "What's there to see in the bazaar? Why not watch your mind instead? That's much more fascinating."

Now that I am older, I find that I agree. Observing how we get caught up in the eight worldly concerns and all the forms of yi midewe ze; experiencing how the wisdom and skillful means of the dharma serve as reliable antidotes; using deep, honest reflection and unconventional thinking to work with our reactions and come to a state of peace—what could be more interesting and exciting? May all who encounter these teachings find them to be similarly engaging and rewarding, and may we all discover the infinite benefits—for ourselves and others—of the practice of patience.

Appendix A
Meditation on Patience

Your meditation cushion—or wherever you go for quiet self-reflection and meditation—is a safe place from which you can go deeper into the practice of patience. It provides a container in which you can build strength outside the heat of a provocative situation. You can use your time on the cushion in many ways. You can go back in time to review what happened after you reacted in a challenging circumstance. You can sort through all that occurred and gain clarity and perspective. From there, you can mentally rehearse how you would like to respond next time. You can also scan your mind for grudges that may be lying dormant. When you discover one of these hidden resentments, you can investigate how it lodged in your being and then apply an effective remedy from these teachings to take care of the problem before it comes out in your actions.

The following is based on a guided meditation I gave during a public talk on patience. It centers on tolerating verbal abuse and rejection. Since we can be provoked in many ways, there can be many variations on this meditation. I hope these instructions will serve as an example of how you can go deeper into the practice of patience from the safety and perspective of your meditation cushion.

First, I request you to generate bodhicitta, the wish to attain enlightenment for the benefit of all sentient beings. This is to establish the supreme motivation at the beginning of the practice.

Now sit up straight in a comfortable position and close your eyes. Pay attention—light attention—to your breathing, in and out. When you realize your mind has drifted off somewhere, simply bring your attention back to your breathing. Come back to this focal point of the breath with a sense of delight, without any self-disparagement or judgment. Just come back and be present with your breath.

Now center yourself in your heart. Make your heart as spacious as possible, as relaxed and joyful as possible. Think of developing patience and get a sense of what that means to you in this moment and overall. To develop patience, you must develop tolerance to raw pain, meaning an ability to be with your experience nakedly, without rejecting anything. Then think of the raw pain caused by someone verbally abusing or criticizing you. Be with that raw pain. You may be tempted to contract, or even to annihilate that experience, but open up and just be with it. You may be tempted to lash out in your mind with aggression, to defend yourself, to say mean things, or to reveal the negative qualities of this person. You may feel betrayed and violently indignant. You may feel confused and even afraid to allow yourself to feel the raw pain without some means of escape or self-protection.

All of these reactions are understandable. But remember your intention: you are giving yourself a chance to practice from the safety of your cushion. You are doing an exercise to develop self-reflection and tolerance so you can learn how to practice genuine patience in the face of real-life challenges. You are doing this to ensure a peaceful heart. So try to resist all temptations to escape or protect yourself, and just be with the raw pain.

Ask yourself: *Can I do this? Is this too difficult? Is there another way that doesn't require tolerating pain? What could that be?* Being with the raw pain may be hard. You may have strong feelings of energy and sensations surging inside your body, with your mind thinking you need to defend yourself. But getting angry, holding a grudge, saying and thinking mean things, getting into a battlefield of who's right (you) and who's wrong (the other person)—does all this help clear the pain that's already there? Or does it add to the pain?

If it doesn't help clear the pain but solidifies it, if your heart becomes more furious, if your mind becomes more active and full of aggressive thoughts, if the pain keeps increasing unbearably, then what is the point of going in that direction? How many times in your life have small sparks turned into big fires in just this way? When that happened, recall how you ended up with not only the original pain, but the added pain of being unable to put out the fire. So why not just be with this small spark of raw pain? Why not let yourself simmer in this experience a bit and be open to what it has to teach you? Isn't this the meaning of tolerance and patience, and isn't this how all great beings before us have practiced and grown? Didn't they all feel these small sparks and use them to develop their tolerance and patience? How else could they have developed as genuine practitioners?

Ask yourself, *Would I rather have patience in my life or be intolerant? Do I want my skin to be as thin as a balloon full of air and my reactions faster than a cobra's, or would I rather have patience? Which will serve me better? Without patience, how will my life be? Can I remain sheltered in a box forever?* Every aspect of your life requires tolerance and patience. If that is so, why not take this great opportunity to develop these qualities further? If tolerating a small spark of pain can bring you complete peace in this life and enlightenment in the future, why not see it as a pain of immunization, a small pain that can save you from much greater pain and bring you health and mental well-being? Why not tolerate it? Why not appreciate this chance, this moment of being completely present with your experience?

Furthermore, doesn't all the pain you experience come from your own karmic deeds in this life or past lives? If you accept this to be true, aren't you ultimately responsible for this pain? Why get angry at or blame someone else? Aren't others acting from the same condition of lacking patience? Aren't they under the influence of their own confusion and intolerance, which has caused them their own pain? Didn't they act that way because they tried to protect themselves from pain? Then why not see that they lack control and are vulnerable, under the influence of their own overwhelming emotions and reacting out of pain? With this in mind, develop some understanding and tolerance toward them. Have compassion for their confused state of mind. Then see if you can also genuinely wish them to be free from their pain and the causes of that pain.

Now reflect even further: *Does this verbal abuse and criticism hurt me physically? Where does it hurt me in my body? By what means? Do words have form? If words have no sharp edges or any other form, how and where do they hurt me?* Maybe you can feel shifting sensations in your body, like a painful tightness in your chest, constriction in your throat, or pressure in your head. Allow these sensations to be there as part of simmering in your raw pain. Notice how these sensations shift and move as you become present with them and then look more deeply at what is happening in your mind. When you feel hurt, notice if that feeling is attached to holding yourself—or something that is an extension of yourself—so extremely dear. Without judgment or rejection, can you sense the self-importance that is at the root of these feelings? Reflect on your deep attachment to yourself and all the various concepts you cling to. Could this be what makes you feel the bulk of your pain?

From the safety of your cushion, muster up the courage to look within and ask yourself these difficult questions. Off the cushion, you will need to do things differently, but here you have the chance to challenge yourself with deep and tender honesty. Realize what a gift this is. Look at the various aspects of your self-importance and how they set you up for insecurity. Investigate which concepts about yourself make you more susceptible to being hurt. Can you see how your attachment to those ideas plays a large part in creating dynamics in your world that often become painful and confusing? Are you able to notice how you feel hurt when those insecurities are poked? How quickly your aggression arises from that feeling of hurt to protect yourself and your ideas? But if you can let go of your attachments to your concepts, won't you be freed from your insecurities as well?

You can accomplish this through practice. But in order to do so, you must first realize the need to self-reflect, to see your self-importance and how strongly you cling to that. This is the best way to stop blaming others and beating yourself up, and instead to take responsibility for your own mind and emotions. So don't come to the defense of that self-importance. Don't go with your usual storylines. Work from within yourself, taking this and similar situations as a means to bring you to a peaceful heart. This practice is indispensable for peace and happiness in this life and for liberation from samsara. So why not change your view, drop your storylines, and simply be with the raw pain?

Be curious about what is really going on inside, underneath the storylines. The only way to get there is by being with the raw pain. After a while you may be surprised at what you find. Look closely at the raw pain. Is it actually "pain," or is it a sensation in your body? If it's a sensation, then just breathe and be present with it. Breathe through the sensation while allowing it to be there. You can even ask the sensation to remain longer. Ask it to make a nice, comfortable home in your heart, so you can develop tolerance and learn everything it has to teach you. Ask it to stay so you can develop renunciation to your self-importance, to your various attachments and aversions, and to samsara in general. The pain can't stay forever, since the sensation is impermanent. But ask it to remain as long as possible, as a special gift to you. Now see what happens to the sensation.

If your mind keeps wondering what to do with the person who caused this pain, think kindly of that person. Realize it is due to them that you have this chance to practice patience and grow. Think compassionately. Wish that they find the happiness they are looking for, the source of happiness they need. Wish that they find freedom from suffering in general and particularly from this karmic situation. Wish that they find peace. Let any thoughts going toward them be kind and compassionate. Wish that this karmic cycle come to an end for them—and for you and all beings. You can let all the energy from your self-discovery go into making prayers and a positive, heartfelt connection with them and with all beings who are in the same boat.

Eventually this process may get you to the point of having nothing to tolerate personally. There is nothing to tolerate when the pain of your self-importance is gone. Once that pain is gone, the sensation also tends to depart. Your whole attitude toward the experience and its cause has changed. This is the magic of your mind, the miracle of your mind, the wisdom of your mind, the skillfulness of your mind. But there are still beings suffering from the kind of confusion you were in, so continue to make prayers that all beings may find the wisdom of the dharma and the freedom of liberation.

Now think of being rejected. Imagine someone rejecting you, without verbal abuse or criticism. Simply imagine being rejected and feel the pain of that. Your state of mind suddenly changes, and all your insecurities surge. You've tried and failed to confirm your own importance through the perceptions of others, and now you feel shaky and uncertain. Now you're desperate for some solid ground to stand on, to solidify yourself as relevant or worthy. Meanwhile, you feel angry and indignant toward the person who rejected you and want to push them away in return.

Be with that pain. Have some perspective on the situation, even some humor—whatever humor you can have. Look at the humor in what you're doing, what you're feeling, how all this is happening. Loosen your mind a bit with humor. First, you want approval, then you want to maintain that esteem indefinitely and even have it increase; when that fails, you want to chuck everyone who rejected you out the window. Doesn't this make your mind feel weak and feeble? So ask yourself, why are you seeking this kind of affection? You don't seek it from everyone, so why seek it from that one particular person? Why them?

Furthermore, what is it that seeks this kind of affection? Is the seeker your wisdom mind or your self-importance? Is your self-importance addicted to seeking such affection and approval from the outside world, even though it has made you suffer so much in the past and keeps on making you suffer? If you don't let go of your self-importance and stop seeking such attention and approval, do you think this suffering will ever stop? Ask yourself, *Do I only know who I am by other people's evaluations?* Instead of depending on others, wouldn't it be better to reflect objectively on your good qualities and develop genuine confidence in your own self-evaluation?

In any case, what do you actually have to gain from seeking this affection and approval, and what do you have to lose? What you gain, in the end, is always pain. What you lose is your freedom to know and evaluate yourself, to have clarity based on your values, principles, and qualities rather than on others' approval and attention. How many times have you made a fool of yourself by seeking attention like this, by trying to be special, to be relevant, or to mean something? How many times have you sold your soul through your grasping to be approved from the outside? How many times have you sold your integrity? How many times have you become a monkey? And who gives you genuine affection when you do this? Does that affection come from true respect or from just seeing right through you? How much pain has all this caused you in the past? Do you still want to continue in this way?

From this point of view, why not cherish being ordinary? All people have enlightened nature. Everyone's hearts are innately imbued with tsewa. Why not cherish what you have in common with all beings rather than make yourself insecure by trying so hard to be special, somehow better than everyone else? If you can enjoy being ordinary, you'll be free from the insidious, unrelenting pain of looking for special attention, affection, and approval from the outside.

Now come back to the sheer pain of rejection. See how it directly punctures your self-importance. You may even have been blind to your self-importance and all its torments until you let yourself feel the pain of rejection. Cherish this pain as a cure for seeking special attention, a remedy for your constant search for approval. Appreciate it as a means of learning the extraordinary contentment of being ordinary. Become the evaluator of yourself and learn to trust your own assessment of how you are. Develop your strength of mind based on selflessness and know the taste of that strength. Work on developing the qualities of your heart based on tsewa.

See this as a chance to start detoxing from your self-importance just by being with this pain, knowing it is a symptom of your addiction and not caused by someone else. See yourself right now in a sort of detox center. Think about the freedom you will gain and the ability to build up your strength genuinely based on your lack of self-importance. This is the freedom to develop qualities based on your good heart and tsewa. It is freedom from being the puppet of others. Now you are taking control of your nose rope* and tying it around your own head.

Again, come back to the pain. This pain is here to teach you a lesson that you must learn in order to become a genuine practitioner, free from ego and from seeking importance. To become a genuine practitioner, you can't only practice when it's convenient. You can't go with the view of dharma only in good times and then revert to conventional wisdom when your self-importance rears its head and you need dharma the most. All pain can teach us a lesson if we are open and ready to learn. So again, see if this pain is actually "pain" or a sensation. Whatever it is, request that it remain until you learn the lesson it has to teach you. Ask it to remain for however long it takes for you to detox. That is your vision. What a gift that is to yourself from your own wisdom mind.

Whatever thoughts and emotions you have toward the person you hold responsible for triggering this pain, let them be kind and compassionate. Don't let the person devalue "you." Instead, turn the tables and willingly devalue yourself, meaning your self-importance. Take this opportunity on your cushion to do the most profound practice of learning, to see through your self-cherishing stance, and come to know the value of devaluing self-importance. What a revolution!

* This refers to the Himalayan method of leading large yaks by ropes tied through their noses.

From here, you can take the seat of being ordinary, humble, and present. When you're no longer concerned or preoccupied with being special, you have no need for the high throne of recognition and approval. You are secure in your good heart and your innate wisdom. Take the low seat from which you can never fall down. From this noble seat, you can stop being so sticky with the world. Be grateful to the person who rejected you for helping you become a more authentic dharma practitioner and a more genuine human being. See humility and ordinariness as the means to tie your nose rope around your own head and never give it to anyone else. This gives you dignity, whether in your family life, your conventional life, or your spiritual life. There is no dignity in being anyone's puppet, especially emotionally speaking. There is no dignity in being emotionally sticky with others. Think of all the great beings who have possessed this kind of humble dignity—what authentic presence they had and have. You can follow in their noble footsteps. The way to do so is to learn this lesson from your own pain.

Now take another look at the pain of rejection. This pain has become very valuable. One rejection gains you freedom from a thousand. A hundred rejections gain you freedom from a million. A thousand rejections gain you freedom from all rejection. You will have no more suffering from rejection. However many rejections you need to go through—one, a hundred, at most a thousand, if you practice in this way—you will become free from its pain. So however long it takes your mind to get free, tolerate this pain with joy. Be patient with it. Have this vision for yourself and for your life.

In any situation where you feel disturbed, use your mind in a similar way. Relate to your emotional disturbance with the wisdom and skillfulness of your mind by being present with the raw experience instead of spiraling outward and downward. This changes your relationship to emotional or mental pain, and you come to experience it as something quite different than how you once did.

Feel confident that you can do this. If it worked this time, why shouldn't it work other times? You just have to spend time with yourself and with this practice on your cushion. Usually you will need to do this after the fact, when you're able to come to this safe space and reflect deeply on what has happened and how you can grow from your experience.

Familiarize yourself and experiment with these meditations to clear your confusion. Use your own creativity to expand your practice and go deeper. Conquering your own intolerance is the true, indispensable warriorship for living in and gaining freedom from samsara.

Now let go of all your concepts. Let go of your whole thinking mind. Let go of the tension of thinking and just be with your present, wakeful mind.

Appendix B

The Seventy-Two Ways We Get Disturbed

Tibetan: yi midewe ze = *"food for mental discontent"*

The eight worldly concerns that stem from our hopes and fears provide the basis for the seventy-two ways we become disturbed.

The Eight Worldly Concerns

HOPING FOR POSITIVE CIRCUMSTANCES

1. Hope for pleasure (physical comfort and mental happiness)
2. Hope for gain (material wealth and prosperity)
3. Hope for praise (heard directly)
4. Hope for a good reputation or fame (in one's society)

FEARING NEGATIVE CIRCUMSTANCES

5. Fear of pain (physical and mental)
6. Fear of loss (material wealth and prosperity)
7. Fear of criticism (heard directly)
8. Fear of having a bad reputation (in one's society)

We all want positive circumstances in our lives and do our best to avoid suffering and pain. These preferences of wanting some things and not wanting others apply to (1) ourselves; (2) those close to us or those we consider an extension of ourselves (family, friends, and associates); and (3) our adversaries (people we dislike or those with whom we are competitive). In each of these three categories, there are four things that we want or hope for, and four things that we don't want or fear. These three categories multiplied by the eight worldly concerns make up twenty-four ways we can become disturbed. These reactions can each occur in relation to the present situation, past events, and future circumstances. Twenty-four ways multiplied by three time frames results in seventy-two—thus, the seventy-two ways.

What We Hope For or Want but Don't Get

We want particular things and circumstances. When we don't get what we want, we generally become discontented or irritated and have the potential to react aggressively and defensively toward anything or anyone that prevents us from fulfilling our desires. We do this in the following thirty-six ways, concerning ourselves, those close to us, and those we dislike in the present, past, and future.

Four ways relative to the **present** that we are disturbed about things concerning **ourselves**:

1. Since I want **physical comfort and mental happiness**, I am disturbed (i.e., irritated, upset, angry, resentful) when something or someone prevents that.
2. Since I want **material wealth and prosperity**, I am disturbed when something or someone prevents that.
3. Since I want to directly hear **praise and positive words**, I am disturbed when something or someone prevents that.
4. Since I want to have a **good reputation**, I am disturbed when something or someone prevents that.

Four ways relative to the **present** that we are disturbed concerning **our close ones**:

5. Since I want them to have **physical comfort and mental happiness**, I am disturbed when something or someone prevents that.

6. Since I want them to have **material wealth and prosperity**, I am disturbed when something or someone prevents that.

7. Since I want them to directly hear **praise and positive words**, I am disturbed when something or someone prevents that.

8. Since I want them to have a **good reputation**, I am disturbed when something or someone prevents that.

Four ways relative to the **present** that we get disturbed concerning **those we dislike:**

9. Since I unconsciously want them to be **physically unwell and mentally unhappy**, I am disturbed when they are happy and well.

10. Since I unconsciously want them to encounter **material loss**, I am disturbed when they have material possessions or wealth.

11. Since I unconsciously want them to be **criticized and hear unpleasant words**, I am disturbed when they are praised or congratulated.

12. Since I unconsciously want them to have **a bad reputation**, I am disturbed when they have a good reputation or are otherwise publicly appreciated.

Four ways relative to the **past** that we become disturbed concerning **ourselves:**

13. I am disturbed that something prevented me from having **physical comfort or mental happiness** in the past.

14. I am disturbed that something prevented me from having **material wealth and prosperity** in the past.

15. I am disturbed that something prevented me from being **praised** in the past.
16. I am disturbed that something prevented me from gaining a **good reputation** in the past.

Four ways relative to the **past** that we become disturbed concerning **our close ones:**

17. I am disturbed that circumstances prevented them from having **physical comfort or happiness** in the past.
18. I am disturbed that circumstances prevented them from having **material wealth and prosperity** in the past.
19. I am disturbed that circumstances prevented them from being **praised** in the past.
20. I am disturbed that circumstances prevented them from having a **good reputation** in the past.

Four ways relative to the **past** that we become disturbed concerning **those we dislike:**

21. I am disturbed by the fact that they were not **physically unwell or mentally unhappy** in the past.
22. I am disturbed by the fact that they did not encounter **material loss** in the past.
23. I am disturbed by the fact that they were not **criticized** in the past.
24. I am disturbed by the fact that they did not have a **bad reputation** in the past.

Four ways relative to the **future** that we become disturbed concerning **ourselves:**

25. I am disturbed by the possibility of **physical discomfort or mental unhappiness.**
26. I am disturbed by the possibility of **material loss or destitution.**

27. I am disturbed by the possibility of being **criticized or blamed.**

28. I am disturbed by the possibility of having a **bad reputation.**

Four ways relative to the **future** that we become disturbed concerning **our close ones:**

29. I am disturbed by the possibility of them becoming **physically unwell or mentally unhappy.**

30. I am disturbed by the possibility of them encountering **material loss or destitution.**

31. I am disturbed by the possibility of them hearing **criticism.**

32. I am disturbed by the possibility of them having a **bad reputation.**

Four ways relative to the **future** that we become disturbed concerning **those we dislike:**

33. I am disturbed by the possibility of them having improved **physical comfort and mental happiness.**

34. I am disturbed by the possibility of them increasing their **wealth and prosperity.**

35. I am disturbed by the possibility of them being **praised.**

36. I am disturbed by the possibility of them enjoying a **good reputation.**

Encountering What We Fear or Do Not Want

Similarly, when we encounter those things we don't want, we become discontent or irritated and have the potential to react aggressively and defensively toward anything or anyone that causes the things we don't want to arise. We do this in the following thirty-six ways concerning ourselves, those close to us, and those we dislike in the present, past, and future.

Four ways relative to the **present** that we get disturbed concerning **ourselves**:

37. I am disturbed (i.e., irritated, upset, angry, resentful) because I don't want to have **physical or mental suffering,** but I do.

38. I am disturbed because I don't want to encounter loss of my **possessions or prosperity,** but I do.

39. I am disturbed because I don't want to be **criticized,** but I am.

40. I am disturbed because I don't want to have a **bad reputation,** but I do.

Four ways relative to the **present** that we get disturbed concerning **our close ones:**

41. I am disturbed because I don't want to them to encounter **physical or mental suffering,** but they do.

42. I am disturbed because I don't want them to encounter **loss of their possessions or prosperity,** but they do.

43. I am disturbed because I don't want them to be **criticized,** but they are.

44. I am disturbed because I don't want them to have a **bad reputation,** but they do.

Four ways relative to the **present** that we get disturbed concerning **those we dislike:**

45. Since I unconsciously don't want them to be **physically well or happy,** I'm disturbed because they are.

46. Since I unconsciously don't want them to be **wealthy or prosperous,** I'm disturbed because they are.

47. Since I unconsciously don't want them to hear **praise and other pleasant words,** I'm disturbed because they do.

48. Since I unconsciously don't want them to have a **good reputation,** I'm disturbed because they do.

Four ways relative to the **past** that we get disturbed concerning **ourselves**:

49. I'm disturbed by the fact that I was **physically unwell or mentally unhappy** in the past.
50. I'm disturbed by the fact that I **lost material wealth or prosperity** in the past.
51. I'm disturbed by the fact that I was **criticized** in the past.
52. I'm disturbed by the fact that I had a **bad reputation** in the past.

Four ways relative to the **past** that we get disturbed concerning **our close ones**:

53. I'm disturbed by the fact that they were **physically unwell or mentally unhappy** in the past.
54. I'm disturbed by the fact that they suffered **material loss** in the past.
55. I'm disturbed by the fact that they endured **criticism** in the past.
56. I'm disturbed by the fact that they had a **bad reputation** in the past.

Four ways relative to the **past** that we get disturbed concerning **those we dislike**:

57. I'm disturbed by the fact that they were **physically well and happy** in the past.
58. I'm disturbed by the fact that they were **wealthy and prosperous** in the past.
59. I'm disturbed by the fact that they were **praised** in the past.
60. I'm disturbed by the fact that they had a **good reputation** in the past.

Four ways relative to the **future** that we get disturbed concerning **ourselves:**

61. I'm disturbed by the possibility of becoming **physically unwell or unhappy.**
62. I'm disturbed by the possibility of **losing my wealth or material resources.**
63. I'm disturbed by the possibility of being **criticized.**
64. I'm disturbed by the possibility of getting a **bad reputation.**

Four ways relative to the **future** that we get disturbed concerning **our close ones:**

65. I'm disturbed by the possibility of them becoming **unwell or unhappy.**
66. I'm disturbed by the possibility of them **losing their wealth or material resources.**
67. I'm disturbed by the possibility of them being **criticized.**
68. I'm disturbed by the possibility of them getting a **bad reputation.**

Four ways relative to the **future** that we get disturbed concerning **those we dislike:**

69. I'm disturbed by the possibility of them becoming **physically well or happy.**
70. I'm disturbed by the possibility of them becoming **wealthy or prosperous.**
71. I'm disturbed by the possibility of them being **praised.**
72. I'm disturbed by the possibility of them gaining a **good reputation.**

Mangala Shri Bhuti

Mangala Shri Bhuti (MSB) is a nonprofit Tibetan Buddhist organization under the direction of Venerable Dzigar Kongtrul Rinpoche. MSB has centers in Colorado, Vermont, Ireland, Brazil, and Japan, which offer programs on introductory and advanced Buddhist topics. Dungse Jampal Norbu, who is Rinpoche's Dharma heir, and Elizabeth Mattis Namgyel, author of *The Power of an Open Question* and *The Logic of Faith*, also teach widely under the umbrella of MSB.

Every Sunday at noon Eastern time, MSB broadcasts the LINK, a live teaching by Rinpoche or one of his students. The LINK podcast contains over 500 talks from the live broadcast. MSB offers online courses led by senior students that introduce key principles of Hinayana, Mahayana, and Vajrayana Buddhism and provide information for those interested in deepening their studies with Dzigar Kongtrul Rinpoche. To learn about any of these teachings and to find out more about Rinpoche and the MSB community, please visit www.mangalashribhuti.org. There you will also find information about the Sangdo Palri Temple of Wisdom and Compassion, the practice of Life Release, making prayer requests, and other topics.